D1637211

MILLENNIAL STUDIES
A Search for Truth

MILLENNIAL STUDIES
A Search for Truth

by
GEORGE L. MURRAY

BAKER BOOK HOUSE
Grand Rapids, Michigan

ISBN: 0-8010-5899-6

Fourth printing, March 1972

PHOTOLITHOPRINTED BY CUSHING - MALLOY, INC.
ANN ARBOR, MICHIGAN, UNITED STATES OF AMERICA
1972

PREFACE

THIS book represents a search for truth on the part of its author. It deals with a phase of Christian truth which has been given no little emphasis in recent years. Fundamentalism, so-called, has been making certain eschatological theories its criterion of orthodoxy. The accredited and recognized theological seminaries have not been taking sufficient cognizance of this fact, with the result that many young ministers have found themselves unable to give intelligent answers to some of the eschatological questions raised by their parishioners. It is probable that they had not arrived at their stated conclusions by any diligent personal investigation, but rather their convictions were those which had been transmitted to them by a former pastor, a trusted friend, or an itinerant evangelist, all of whom had likely received them in the same manner.

Few laymen find it possible to devote much time to a study of theology. Other occupations and interests would make this impossible, even if one possessed the necessary facilities and the preliminary requirements for such a study. This makes it all the more necessary for the Christian minister to ascertain, and make known, what the Word of God teaches on every phase of Christian doctrine.

The author of this book has for twelve years ministered to a city congregation of Bible believers who do not see eye to eye on questions of eschatology. Requests for sermons on this subject had to be ignored for a long time. While the truth of the Lord's return was held tenaciously, and frequently referred to, it was only after the subject had been studied for about ten years that a definite conclusion was reached and a definite position taken.

No apology is made for this delay. A clear doctrine of eschatology is not urgently necessary to the salvation of man, and that is the Christian minister's first concern. Eschatology is also a subject on which men of keen intellects, scholarly attainments, and deep spirituality have greatly disagreed. In such a matter, it is not a mark of superior wisdom to reach conclusions hastily. It is true that there are many people of quite ordinary mental and spiritual equipment who insist that eschatology is as clear to them as the noonday light, and who have not found it necessary to give the matter any serious study. We shall not be too greatly moved by any adverse criticism from such sources. The eschatological skein is one not easily disentangled.

This work does not pretend to answer all the questions; but it does represent what the author considers a satisfactory eschatological position, reached by an earnest and diligent study of the Word of God. The reader is requested to read the book through before passing judgment upon it, and then to pronounce a sentence based upon the evidence of Scripture, showing it to be right or wrong. The evidence of Scripture must consist of the whole sum and substance of revealed truth, and not texts isolated from their context.

The author does not quite expect that all his friends will agree with the views expressed in these pages, because views to the contrary have come to be rather widely accepted in recent years. It is profitable to examine all interpretations of truth in the light of the truth itself. If our accepted creedal dogmas have the support and sanction of Holy Scripture, a re-examination of them will but strengthen our faith. Truth never fears light. If we have been accepting as truth a human opinion not in harmony with the Divine revelation, it is beneficial to make that discovery.

There are few truths which have not had to run the gauntlet of controversy, and many truths are in our possession today because there happened to be men who, while they loved peace, would not part with conviction at the price of peace. They were brave enough to leave beaten tracks in search of truth; and finding it, they were not to be frightened out of their possession of it by criticism and condemnation from those who feared its impact.

In this volume considerable attention has been given to the dispensational theory of an earthly Palestinian kingdom. This was made necessary by the fact that it is the main plank in the erroneous platform of dispensationalism. It goes without saying, of course, that however much we disagree with the dispensationalist's eschatology, we hail and love as brethren all who have found salvation at the Cross, and who love our Lord Jesus Christ in sincerity and truth.

Those who know the author personally will bear testimony to his aversion to contention and controversy. The purpose of this book is not to create controversy, but to establish truth. That the writing of the book was undertaken in the midst of a strenuous pastorate might explain at least some of its blemishes. It has involved much study of dispensational and prophetic literature, as well as a rather thorough examination of the Bible. Much interesting material has had to be eliminated, due to restrictions of space. If the book has any merit, the praise belongs to the "Father of lights," Who has been pleased to illumine difficult passages along the way. It is hoped that a reading of it will create greater interest in a study of the Bible, and help pilgrims on the way to the Celestial City.

It is but fitting that acknowledgment should be made of the help received from the writings of other men, some known and some unknown. Permission to quote copyrighted works has been kindly given by Fleming H. Revell Company, New York City; Zondervan Publishing House, Grand Rapids, Michigan; Bible Truth Depot, Swengel, Pennsylvania; Hamilton Brothers, Boston, Massachusetts; Professor Oswald Allis of Philadelphia, Pennsylvania; and Rev. J. Marcellus Kik of Montreal, Canada.

My thanks are due my friends who have read the manuscript and offered valuable suggestions, thus aiding and encouraging me in my search for truth.

G. L. M.

Newton, Massachusetts

CONTENTS

Chapter I.

General Considerations

THERE are few ministers of the Gospel who have not at some time experienced a conflict between duty and inclination. Whatever may be said of Christian courage, we do not readily disagree with those whom we love. It may, therefore, be a temptation to remain silent about our convictions while in the fellowship of those who do not share our views. The communication of truth is not usually promoted by silence, however, and there are times when the interests of truth and justice may demand an expression of our convictions. Such expressions, while involving differences of opinion, do not prove lack of charity or the absence of Christian love. It is a matter of common knowledge that the apostle who wrote the thirteenth chapter of first Corinthians on the subject of love was the same apostle who said, "But when Peter was come to Antioch, I withstood him to the face, because he was to be blamed" (Galatians 2:11). We are well aware that what we write here will not be in accord with what many of our friends believe; but we deny to them the right to be angry at us, as we deny to ourselves the right to be angry at them for what they believe. It is questionable whether we can count on that consideration, but our trepidation at these thoughts is not unmixed with the hope that God may bless this humble effort to His own glory, and that we may have the added compensation of extracting jewels of truth from the debris and wreckage of controversies by which the truth has been frequently obscured, though not destroyed.

When the apostles went out preaching the Gospel of salvation their announcement was ". . . that Christ died for our sins according to the Scriptures; and that He was buried and that He rose again the third day according to the Scriptures"

11

(I Corinthians 15:3-4). Their emphasis was on the fact that Christ has come into the world to atone for human guilt, "For Christ also hath once suffered for sins, the just for the unjust, that He might bring us to God . . ." (I Peter 3:18). This also was the burden of the preacher's message in the post-apostolic age. The so-called "Dark Ages" lost sight of it, but the Protestant reformers re-discovered and revived it, preaching and teaching that justification was by faith, that salvation was all of grace, and that there was but one plan of salvation for both Jew and Gentile.

A new day has come upon us. It is not now sufficient to preach Christ and Him crucified, but orthodoxy must include the ability to chart the future according to well defined dispensational lines. Some Bible conferences, Christian organizations, and religious periodicals make it mandatory by their constitutions that their officers believe in the premillennial return of the Lord Jesus Christ. This would seem to condition Christian fellowship upon a certain eschatological viewpoint, and to designate that particular point of view as the last word in orthodoxy.

This premillennialism is not the Chiliasm of the early Church, but something which first appeared early in the nineteenth century. It is a premillennialism wedded to dispensationalism.

All premillennialists do not accept extreme dispensationalism. Many devout students of the Word of God, having the conviction that there shall be no earthly millennium prior to the Lord's return, accept premillennialism as the only alternative to postmillennialism which they consider to be unwarranted by Scripture. Extreme dispensationalism is different. It speaks of two Gospels: the Gospel of Grace, and the Gospel of the Kingdom. It has one message for the Jew and another for the Gentile. Just recently we listened to a Christian minister announcing to the Jews that the moment was imminent when they should be regathered to Palestine to enjoy an era of prosperity unparalleled in the days of David and Solomon. While this promise was being given the Jews, the speaker urged his Gentile hearers to read and study John 3:16.

The origin of this new gospel is not difficult to trace. It came into prominence through the instrumentality of John Nelson Darby, a British Episcopalian clerygman, who was born in 1800 and died in 1882, one of the early leaders of the sect called the Plymouth Brethren. The doctrines of John Darby were popularized in America by the Rev. Charles Ingersoll Scofield. Dr. Scofield, born in 1843, entered the legal profession and was a practicing lawyer at the time of his conversion in the thirty-sixth year of his age. Three years later he abandoned the practice of law to enter the Christian ministry and was ordained by a Congregational Council, which did not require any formal theological training on his part. Many years later, Dr. Scofield, with the assistance of an editorial board consisting of devoted Christian leaders, produced what has been called the *Scofield Reference Bible*. This Bible contains the King James version of the Bible with a system of chain references and footnotes setting forth the doctrines of John Darby, which had been assiduously absorbed and zealously propagated by Dr. Scofield, who, while rejecting Darby's ecclesiology, accepted his eschatology in its totality.

The popularity of the Scofield Reference Bible may be learned from the fact that over two million copies have been sold since it first appeared. It has done more than any other medium in promoting dispensationalism in America. This Bible offers to any casual student of Scripture a general idea of the order of eschatological events from the first to the second advent of Jesus Christ, and supplies that knowledge with minimum effort and time. Dr. T. T. Shields of Toronto, an outstanding and militant Baptist minister, says, "From a point of entire ignorance of Scripture to the position of oracular religious certainty, especially respecting eschatological matters, for some people requires from three to six months with a Scofield Bible."[1]

Let it be said here that we believe whole-heartedly that Dr. Scofield was a man of great piety and genuine sincerity. He could not be accused of any departure from the great cardinal doctrines of the Christian faith. His emphasis on such doctrines as regeneration, the new birth, and the atonement deserves acknowledgment and admiration. This can also be said of many who share his dispensational views, and in no school of Christian thought can one find less liberalism than among the premillennialists. It is to be remembered, however, that there are times when in attempting to keep out of the ditch on one side of the road, we may go over too far to the opposite side, and fare no better. We have the conviction that Dr. Scofield has done this, and we believe that now seeing no longer "through a glass darkly" he would not object to any endeavor to rectify what is manifestly unscriptural in his teachings. It is not, therefore, with any lack of Christian charity that we express the conviction that the Scofield Reference Bible teaches eschatological doctrines which are at variance with what was taught and written by the prophets and apostles of God. These spurious doctrines are set forth in declarative and positive statements, admitting no suggestion of any interpretation that differs with Dr. Scofield's. In fact, the reader would not gather from Dr. Scofield's notes that any of his doctrines were open to question, or that there was any other opinion in existence. This was excellent psychology, employed to teach bad theology.

We believe that this theology constitutes a real challenge to the Christian church in our day. The only remedy lies in a better knowledge of the Word of God, systematized doctrinal preaching, and proper catechetical instruction. To be sure, the key to a real knowledge of Scripture lies in a personal experience, by which the spirit within man shall respond to the spirit

---

(1) Shields, T. T., THE GOSPEL WITNESS, April 7, 1932

which permeates the Word. Those possessing such a key can enter into the storehouses of Divine truth to their own spiritual enrichment. One can hardly suppress the tendency to wonder whether we ministers seek to become specialists in politics and economics and in the solving of social problems, rather than the stewards of the manifold grace and absorbing mysteries of the Word of God. Our preoccupation with secondary generalities is one of the reasons why so many of us have never formed any personal convictions on some of the great doctrines of the Word of God, and particularly on the subject of eschatology, and the Lord's return. Better acquaintance with the Bible in its entirety, and a proper understanding of the sum total of its teachings would have enabled us to avert many of our modern tangents.

In addition to our acquaintance with the Bible itself, it is profitable to consult the findings of those who have made a scholarly and exhaustive study of it. In this connection one thinks of the great Westminster Assembly of Divines, probably representing greater theological learning than any other Assembly before or since. This momentous conclave could not find in the Word of God the things which men profess to see so plainly in our day. The Westminster Assembly linked up the Lord's return with the general resurrection and the judgment, but nowhere in their conclusions can one find a place for the interjection of one thousand years of earthly bliss. Their interpretation leaves room for only the amillennial eschatological position.

The theological confusion of our day, as well as the unrest of the time, calls for clear, unambiguous teaching on the subject of eschatology. What would seem to be the ominous signs of the approaching end of the age are so conspicuous that many Christians are anxious to know more of the Divine plan.

In addition to this reasonable anxiety, nature itself seems to have endowed men with a generous measure of curiosity concerning things to come. It is upon this natural curiosity that palmists, fortune tellers, and clairvoyants build their lucrative business. It is, therefore, not surprising that people who can give a semblance of religious color and sanction to their speculations can quickly gain a following of those who are not too well grounded in the truth. Christian ministers may choose to ignore discussing such subjects, but our silence will not contribute to orthodoxy on the part of our people. It is only by the assimilation of knowledge that men are fortified against untruths and half truths. Reluctance on the part of the Christian pulpit to discuss these matters has frequently left seekers after truth at the mercy of those who have capitalized upon their inadequate knowledge and lack of qualifications to analyze what was offered in the name of truth. Devout and well-intentioned men and women frequently find their way into circles in which prophetic speculations are convincingly presented and therefore accepted without question. Children playing with matches find that pastime so enjoyable that they are willing to renounce safety in exchange for light with disastrous results sometimes. Church people have played this game too, with similar consequences. There can be little question but that the church by its neglect of certain phases of truth has contributed largely to the mushroom growth of an endless variety of cults claiming to satisfy the yearnings of seekers for truth. This neglect is inexcusable, inasmuch as it is not impossible to ascertain what is plainly revealed in the Scriptures.

In this work, we hope to examine all too briefly what the Bible teaches regarding the second advent of Christ, its manner and the events associated with it. There are portions of Scripture to which one can hardly give any interpretation other than that of an impersonal and invisible return. We might also digress to say there are some passages which are generally accepted as referring to our Lord's personal return but which are legitimately capable of a different interpretation. An example of this may be found in Matthew 10:23: "And when they persecute you in this city, flee ye into another, for verily

I say unto you, ye shall not have gone over the cities of Israel till the Son of Man be come." Dr. Scofield states that this passage "has in view the preaching of the remnant in the tribulation preceding the return of Christ in glory."[2] Dr. G. Campbell Morgan, on the other hand, expresses the conviction that "This coming of the Son of Man" can be explained only in the sense of judgment, which judgment fell on Jerusalem in 70 A. D. "Who shall say," asks Dr. Morgan, "that in His personal form He did not guide the Roman legions as they took Jerusalem?"[3] While we respect the views of such eminent men, we feel inclined to disagree with them in this connection. We find the instructions given by our Lord to the disciples on this occasion corresponding exactly to those given to the seventy as reported in Luke 10. The evangelist, Luke, seems to throw light on what is meant by the coming of the Son of Man in this case, for he says, "After these things the Lord appointed other seventy also, and sent them two and two before His face into every city and place, whither He Himself would come" (Luke 10:1). It was the evident intention of Jesus Christ "to come" to the cities of Israel with the gospel. Matthew tells us that "Jesus went about all the cities and villages teaching in their synagogues and preaching the gospel of the kingdom" (Matthew 9:35). Luke tells us also of another occasion when Jesus said, "I must preach the kingdom of God to other cities also; for therefore am I sent" (Luke 4:43). We believe that the foregoing furnishes an example of the tendency to read the Lord's return into passages which may not have any real bearing upon that phase of truth. We do not believe that the above passage has any reference to the "preaching of the remnant in the tribulation," nor even to the Lord's personal return.

It is not to be denied that the Lord came in a very true sense at the destruction of Jerusalem and supervised that dreadful judgment, but we do not accept that coming as the ultimate fulfillment of the promises of His final return.

(2)   Scofield, C. I., THE SCOFIELD REFERENCE BIBLE, Page 1009
(3)   Morgan, G. C., THE GOSPEL ACCORDING TO MATTHEW, Page 106

There are those who say that the promise of the Lord's return was fulfilled at Pentecost when the Holy Spirit descended upon the infant church. It may be remembered in this connection that the Lord had promised not to leave His disciples comfortless. He said, "I will come to you." On that occasion He was speaking of the Comforter and identifying Himself in essence with the Holy Spirit. The Spirit is in the church and in a very real sense "the Lord is that Spirit." At the same time, if language has any meaning, the church of Jesus Christ is entitled to believe that the day is coming when He shall return personally and when we shall see Him face to face. He and His inspired apostles give promises to this effect, which can hardly lend themselves to any other interpretation.

We cannot imagine that it was either the fall of Jerusalem, or the day of Pentecost, or the death of the individual Christian, or the conversion of any souls, or any of those events by which some men seek to explain the Lord's return, that Paul had in mind when he said, "For the Lord Himself shall descend from heaven with a shout, with the voice of the archangel, and with the trump of God: and the dead in Christ shall rise first: then we which are alive and remain shall be caught up together with them in the clouds, to meet the Lord in the air" (I Thessalonians 4:16-17). In this connection the apostle used "great plainness of speech," and his words are scarcely capable of being misunderstood. It is evident that he was thinking of the Lord's personal return for His people at the end of the age.

At the moment of Christ's ascension, the disciples were assured by two heavenly messengers that "this same Jesus, which is taken up from you into heaven, shall come in like manner as ye have seen Him go into heaven" (Acts 1:11). No subsequent Divine intervention in human affairs can be accepted as the fulfillment of this prediction. He has not yet come "in like manner" in a visible, personal form. If with some we say that this was fulfilled at Pentecost, we must face the fact that the men who were intimately familiar with all that occurred at Pentecost were the very men who still looked for the "glorious appearing of our Lord and Saviour Jesus Christ." The writers of the Acts, of the Epistles, and the Revelation, mention the return of the Lord about 150 times in which His return is referred to as being in the future. This does not deny His presence in the church at this moment. His promise, "Lo, I am with you always," is being fulfilled daily in the experiences of His people, as is "Where two or three are gathered together in My name, there am I in the midst of them" (Matthew 18:20).

This was true in the days of the apostles when the scoffers were mocking and asking, "Where is the promise of His coming?" Peter did not insist that the Lord had already returned at the destruction of Jerusalem, or on the day of Pentecost. He pointed out that the Lord's coming was being delayed in order to give men all the necessary opportunity for repentance. Said he, "The Lord is longsuffering to us-ward, not willing that any should perish" (II Peter 3:9). Peter anticipated the day when in a cataclysmic upheaval the Lord should return.

We are sometimes told that it is unnecessary for Him to return and therefore unreasonable for us to expect the return of One who is never absent. That He is never absent from His own is a matter in which His people rejoice, but that there is a sense in which He is absent is emphasized by every evangelical observance of the Lord's Supper. That sacred ordinance is administered with the familiar words of institution, "For as often as ye eat this bread, and drink this cup, ye do show the Lord's death till He come." If He is already here, in every sense in which He will ever be here, these words have no meaning. At this point it should be understood that we are not referring or subscribing to the current belief of a thousand years' reign in Jerusalem. We have never been able to see the purpose of such a reign, nor can we understand how the Lord's physical presence, visible to a comparatively small number of His people, could mean more that His spiritual presence experienced by them all, unless we choose to dispense with faith and walk by sight. Our insistence is upon the ancient faith of the Christian church that "now once in the end of the age hath He put away sin by the sacrifice of Himself . . . and unto them that look for Him shall He appear the second time without sin unto salvation" (Hebrews 9:26, 28).

It cannot be denied that the Scriptures differentiate between our Lord's spiritual presence in the church now, and His visible, physical return from heaven at the end of the age. The man Christ Jesus is now physically and corporeally at the right hand of God where He was seen by Stephen and the Seer of Patmos. The early church believed that He would come back from heaven to earth at the end of the age and that every eye should see Him. This view is reflected in the historic creeds of the church. In the Apostles' Creed, which in its earliest form comes to us from the middle of the second century, the early church expressed its faith regarding the return of Christ, stating that the crucified Lord Who rose from the dead on the third day, and sat on the right hand of God, shall return from thence to judge the quick and the dead. The early church rejoiced in the hope of His appearing and in the prospect of that day when His people shall be like Him and shall see Him as He is. This is the desire of the true church in every age. He has not yet come in all His glory. Men in their mortal bodies could not endure the vision of that glory. During His earthly life His glory was veiled and only this made it possible for men to look upon Him. When the law was given on Mt. Sinai "so terrible was the sight, that Moses said, I exceedingly fear and quake" (Hebrews 12:21). The words of Paul are to the point here: "If the ministration of condemnation be glory, much more doth the ministration of righteousness exceed in glory. For even that which was made glorious had no glory in this respect, by reason of the glory that excelleth" (II Corinthians 3:9-10). While this passage contrasts grace with law, its words may well apply to the coming of the Son of God, Who said that He should come in all His glory and all His holy angels with Him. It was a little of this glory that was unveiled to the disciples on the Mount of Transfiguration and which proved too much for them. It was a beam of this glory that blinded the Man of Tarsus on the Damascus road and which he frequently described as "a light from heaven, above the brightness of the sun." It was this glory that caused John, on the Isle of Patmos, to fall down at His feet as one dead; "His countenance was as the sun shineth in his strength" (Revelation 1:16). It is this glory that is described as "the brightness of His coming"; and it shall be impossible for anyone to remain unaware of it when it happens, "For the Son of Man shall come in the glory of His Father with His angels" (Matthew 16:27).

The following chapters endeavor to show something of the Scriptural panorama of events leading up to the Lord's return, as well as to present an evaluation of the varied opinions and theories held by Christians on this fascinating subject. It was this great variety, with the confusion and bewilderment which they engendered, that drove us to make a careful search of Scripture in order to find a solid standing-place for our own feet. We believe that our search has confirmed us in that faith which is the ancient heritage of the Christian church — the belief that the Lord Jesus Christ will return from heaven to judge the world at the end of the age, that His resurrected church will rise to meet Him as a bride adorned for her husband, and the saints who are spared the experience of dying shall be changed so that their bodies will correspond in substance with the bodies of those raised from the dust of the earth. This is the happy day that will bring deliverance to the groaning creation, that shall see death swallowed up in victory, the day in which the Lord Jehovah shall wipe away all tears from His people's eyes, the day for which His church is longing and saying, "Even so come, Lord Jesus."

Chapter 2.

God's Covenant with Abraham

WHEN the unknown stranger joined the sorrowing disciples on the Emmaus Road, "Beginning at Moses and all the prophets, He expounded unto them in all the scriptures the things concerning Himself" (Luke 24:27). He was the central theme of Moses and the prophets. His day brought rejoicing to their hearts as they saw it afar off. This should be kept in mind in view of the prevailing tendency on the part of many people to subordinate the contents of the Old Testament to a fancied vision of a political Palestinian kingdom which many suppose shall be established in these latter days and shall be one of the certain antecedents of the Lord's return. The undue emphasis placed on positive prophetic declarations by those who profess to understand prophecy does not always make for stability in Christian faith.

People whose hopes are often incited to expect the fulfillment of what they accept as prophecy are equally disappointed when their hopes do not materialize. The result is that some lose faith in the Scriptures, rather than in those who undertake to interpret them. We have heard one such interpreter foretelling with plainness of speech how the recent world war would end, and claiming Scriptural support for his convictions, which, however, did not come true. We gasped as we listened to a speaker of wide reputation telling a Bible Conference that God brought about the defeat of the Churchill government and the election of a Labor government in order to open Palestine for the Jews, "God's chosen people." An audible "Amen" emanated from the audience when he buttressed his statements by saying, "It is all in the Book," although no quotation from the Book was given.

Our astonishment at exegetical extravagance reached a high point recently when we heard a radio preacher interpreting the first verse of Isaiah 53, "Who hath believed our report? and to whom is the arm of the Lord revealed?," as the voice of the Jewish "remnant" during the "Great Tribulation." Evidence that this opinion is widespread may be adduced from the following statement by a recent writer: "Isaiah 53 may be applied to all sinners, but its interpretation shows us that Isaiah is speaking of the confession of the nation Israel in a coming day."[1] The Holy Spirit gives an entirely different interpretation of this passage in John 12:37, 38. "But though He had done so many miracles before them, yet they believed not on Him: That the saying of Esaias the prophet might be fulfilled, which he spake, Lord, who hath believed our report, and to whom hath the arm of the Lord been revealed?"

We give these as samples of prophetic interpretations to which American audiences are being treated today and which are being preached and parrotted from one person to another, forming a system of religious thought which, like the proverbial snowball, has assumed the proportions of a religious avalanche, sweeping everything out of its way. Evangelicals who express concern that people are turning away their ears from the truth and giving heed to fables would do well to make sure that we are not partakers of this evil and not in any way responsible for it. If evangelicals complain that liberals rob the Word of God of the meaning which God has meant it to convey, it may well be feared that literalists are guilty of adding to it what God has not put into it; and, while claiming to be fundamentalists and evangelicals, they may be equally blameworthy in the sight of God. The plagues mentioned in the book of Revelation are pronounced upon those adding to the Word of God, as well as upon those taking from it (Revelation 22:18, 19). It is, therefore, a most serious responsibility to interpret the Word of God, not only from the standpoint of the effect of our

---

(1) Feinberg, Chas. L., PREMILLENNIALISM AND AMILLENNIALISM, Page 33

interpretation upon others, but from the standpoint of our own individual responsibility as stewards of the grace of God.

The purpose of this chapter is to examine the terms of God's covenant with Abraham in order to ascertain whether or not it promises final possession of Palestine by the Hebrew people. The answer to our inquiry is important not only to Jews, but also to Christians, especially to the great body of Christians who regard this as an integral part of a system of Biblical interpretation. If the theory collapses under the scrutiny of investigation, its collapse will undermine human confidence in the other intricate eschatological theories interwoven and associated with it. In this inquiry the Scriptures must be our supreme court of appeal. A highly dispensational book open before us directs our attention to Genesis 12:7: "And the Lord appeared unto Abram, and said, Unto thy seed will I give this land." Our author says, "There is the first promise. It is very sure and very clear. There are no conditions made."[2] Let the reader visualize the circumstances in which Abraham had been placed. He had come into a land in which he was a stranger, and as if to remind us of certain besetting dangers, the Word of God says, "The Canaanite was then in the land" (Genesis 12:6). It was a comfort for Abraham to have Divine assurance that he could not be dispossessed. In addition to the Canaanite menace, there was also a famine in the land; and it was sufficiently severe to drive Abraham into the land of Egypt. In Egypt he prospered, but was driven away when his misrepresentation of facts concerning Sarai, his wife, became known. He emerged from Egypt once again and in Genesis 13:1-17 we find God amplifying the former promise: "Lift up now thine eyes, and look from the place where thou art northward, and southward, and eastward, and westward. For all the land which thou seest, to thee will I give it, and to thy seed forever . . . Arise, walk through the land in the length of it and in the breath of it; for I will give it unto thee." It should be plainly

---

(2) Ironside, Harry A., THE LAMP OF PROPHECY, Page 72

understood that God is allaying Abraham's fears by the assurance that neither he nor his seed shall be dispossessed by the inhabitants of the land.

The literalist reminds us of the word "forever" which to him is the allimportant word here. We are frequently reminded that the "forever" must mean " FOR EVER." This is not without difficulty even for the literalist. Man's tenure of any part of the earth is not permanent. "It is appointed unto man once to die and after that the judgment." His leases and contracts in material possessions must come to an end. What, then, does God mean? What would Abraham understand by the word "forever"? If a man is threatened with eviction from his home and a friend of proven ability, to implement his promises, will give him a promise that he shall possess that home forever, how shall he interpret those words? He will not expect to live there eternally. The most he could expect from the promise would be that he should spend his natural life there and that his dust should rest there after death. This was what God plainly promised and fulfilled to Abraham. He possessed the land of Canaan in every sense in which a man can possess a land. The writer of the Epistle to the Hebrews says, "By faith he sojourned in the land of promise, as in a strange country, dwelling in tabernacles with Isaac and Jacob, the heirs with him of the same promise: For he looked for a city which hath foundations, whose builder and maker is God" (Hebrews 11:9-10). This passage should throw a revealing light on the whole picture. Abraham, confessing himself to be a stranger there, looked for "a better country." At the same time, he and his seed, Isaac and Jacob, possessed the land of Canaan as long as they lived. There was a time when Jacob left Canaan to go down into Egypt, but that was done at Divine behest. God commanded him to go down and promised that He would bring him up again. There is ample proof to be adduced from the Word that God fulfilled to Abraham and to Abraham's seed the promise that they should possess Canaan. Today, the ashes of Abraham, Isaac and Jacob mingle with the soil of the "Cave of the field of Machpelah before Mamre . . . in the land of Canaan," which Abraham bought "for a possession of a burying place." He possessed Canaan during his earthly life, and his ashes rest in Canaan until the resurrection. The same can be said of his seed, Isaac and Jacob, "The heirs with him of the same promise." Surely God has fulfilled his promise to Abraham to give him and his seed a permanent place in the land.

The next promise to Abraham concerning Canaan is so plain in all its implications that anyone with a cursory acquaintance with the Old Testament can understand it. In Genesis 15:13-14, we read that God said unto Abraham, "Know of a surety that thy seed shall be a stranger in a land that is not theirs, and shall serve them; and they shall afflict them four hundred years; And also that nation, whom they shall serve, will I judge: and afterward shall they come out with great substance." Anyone possessing a mere Sunday School knowledge of Scripture will readily see that this refers to the bondage of Israel in Egypt and subsequent exodus. This description of the exodus is followed by a covenant on the part of God to give to the seed of Abraham the land of Canaan "from the river of Egypt unto the great river, the river Euphrates" (Genesis 15:18). This covenant does not include the word "forever" although it is contended by some that its full terms are yet to be fulfilled, and that the Israelites have never possessed the land to the extent described here. Happily, the Word of God gives the true and final answer here, too. We invite our readers to turn to I Kings 4:21, 24 where we read: "And Solomon reigned over all kingdoms from the river (the Euphrates) unto the land of the Philistines, and unto the border of Egypt . . . For he had dominion over all the region on this side the river, from Tiphsah even to Assah, over all the kings on this side the river; and he had peace on all sides round about him."

We now return, momentarily, to Genesis 15:18 where the Lord promised Abraham that his natural seed should inherit the land of Canaan, which promise we have shown to have been literally fulfilled. God promised that in the accomplishment of this purpose the seed of Abraham would subdue the Kenites, and the Kenizzites, and the Kadmonites, and the Hittites, and the Perizzites, and the Rephaims, and the Amorites, and the Canaanites, and the Girgashites, and the Jebusites. (See Genesis 15:19-21.) The dispensationalist who still insists that this is to be fulfilled at the end of the gospel dispensation will have to face the difficulty of resurrecting and reconstituting these ancient nations in order that his returning Israel may subdue them. He can, however, escape this impossible task by following the Word of God, for if we turn to the ninth chapter of the book of Joshua, we find these very nations mentioned once again. The nations which God mentioned to Abraham many years before, "the Hittite, and the Amorite, and the Canaanite, the Perizzite, the Hivite, and the Jebusite" appear and gather themselves together in a league to "fight with Joshua and Israel with one accord" (Joshua 9:1-2). All this should not only throw light on our mistaken man-made theories, but should also confirm our faith in the marvelous Word of God and His faithfulness to His promises.

It is interesting in this connection to look at the testimony of Joshua which we believe ought to be conclusive: "And the Lord gave unto Israel ALL the land which He sware to give unto their fathers; and they possessed it, and dwelt therein . . . There failed not ought of any good thing which the Lord had spoken unto the house of Israel, ALL CAME TO PASS" (Joshua 21:43, 45). The law of evidence is certainly on the side of Joshua as against the modern dispensationalist. It remains for us to touch only upon the promises of God to Abraham as contained in Genesis 17. We are frequently reminded by the dispensationalist that this is a Covenant of Grace, and also an Everlasting Covenant. To both assertions we breathe a fervent "Amen." The Covenant of Grace which God was revealing to Abraham and which in time to come was to be ratified by the blood of Jesus Christ of the seed of Abraham is described for us in the Epistle to the Hebrews, where it is said: "For if that first covenant had been faultless, then should no place have been sought for the second. For finding fault with them, He saith, Behold the days come, saith the Lord, when I will make a new covenant with the house of Israel and with the house of Judah . . . For this is the covenant that I will make with the house of Israel after those days, saith the Lord: I will put my laws into their mind, and write them in their hearts: and I will be to them a God and they shall be to me a people" (Hebrews 8:7, 8, 10). This is the New Testament description of the Covenant of Grace and there is no word of the possession of land or material goods in it. This is the Everlasting Covenant as the reader may ascertain for himself. There can be no everlasting covenant concerning material possessions, for no material possessions are in themselves everlasting.

We have to confess that it is with something of a shudder that we listen to men declaring with absolute dogmatism that God has yet to fulfill His promises to Abraham. We believe that this is an affront to God in which Abraham would not willingly participate. Let us consult the record. Many, many years after Abraham finished his earthly pilgrimage and had gone to be with God, we find the faithful Nehemiah bearing witness to the fact that God was faithful in fulfilling His covenant with Abraham. Let us hear his evidence: "Thou art the Lord the God, Who didst choose Abram, and broughtest him forth out of Ur of the Chaldees, and gavest him the name of Abraham; And foundest his heart before thee and madest a covenant with him to give him the land of the Canaanites, the Hittites, and the Amorites, and the Perizzites and the Jebusites, and the Girgashites, to give it I say to his seed, AND HAST PERFORMED THY WORDS; For Thou art righteous" (Nehemiah

9:7, 8). Could any words be clearer than these? They are the words of one conversant with the history of his people. Whatever political movements we may witness now or in the future by way of a restoration of Hebrew economy in the land of Palestine, these will not come by way of fulfillment of God's promises to Abraham of possession of the land, for we have conclusive evidence that these promises have been fulfilled. The dispensationalist cannot build a case on the assumption that God's promises to Abraham have to be fulfilled, for Scripture clearly states that they have already had their fulfillment.

Chapter 3.

The Interpretation of Prophecy

IN the previous chapter we have shown how God's promises to Abraham were literally fulfilled. God was speaking to him of the possession of Canaan by himself and his natural seed. In addition, God was giving him dim foreshadowings of the Covenant of Grace which would apply to his spiritual seed. It is essential to our understanding of Scripture that we should remember that God dealt first with the natural seed of Abraham, who constituted the Hebrew people, the chosen nation. With that nation's rejection of Christ, it ceased to be God's peculiar treasure and now God's Israel consists of all believers in the Lord Jesus Christ. Of them the apostle Peter speaks as "a chosen generation, a royal priesthood, an holy nation, a peculiar people" (I Peter 2:9). All this must have a bearing upon our interpretation of the prophetic Scriptures, and is a part of the line of demarcation separating dispensationalism from other systems of eschatology. The dispensationalist insists that the Old Testament prophets have nothing to say about the New Testament church, but that their theme is an earthly Palestinian kingdom, whose capital will be Jerusalem, in which Jesus Christ will reign for a thousand years, occupying the material throne of David and compelling the world to live righteously.

The available records of God's dealings with His people from the beginning do not reveal any proof or precedent for the idea that twenty centuries of this dispensation of grace should have been hidden by God from all the Old Testament prophets, nor do we believe that Bible study will prove this idea to be Scriptural. At this stage we should like to give our readers the most definite assurance of our high personal regard for Christian brethren who disagree with us in matters of eschatology, and whose words we must quote here. Many of them have been used mightily in the winning of souls. Some of them we have invited to our pulpit because we do not think it necessary to their proclamation of the Gospel that they should agree with our eschatological position. We only claim the right to express our views as publicly as they express theirs, if perhaps we do it with less dogmatism. This freedom is a recognized privilege among Christians who do not regard any mortal man as being infallible.

One leading evangelical minister says, "I do not find any prophecy that has to do particularly with the Christian dispensation as such. Prophecy has to do largely with God's dealings with His earthly people, Israel, and with the great Gentile nations."[1] Elsewhere the same minister writes of the present Gospel age as a parenthesis and states that "the moment the Messiah died the prophetic clock stopped. There has not been a tick upon that clock for nineteen centuries. It will not begin to go again until the entire present age has come to an end and Israel will once more be taken up by God."[2] The same views are expressed by another writer, who, speaking of the Old Testament prophets says, "Upon the horizon of their outlook there loomed large the two advents of the king, the one for the purpose of suffering for the sin of the world, and the other for the purpose of reigning as the Son of David upon his throne. Any intervening period was foreign to them because it was not revealed to them by God." Again the same writer follows the path familiar to men of this persuasion and says that "the clock of God stopped at the end of the sixty-ninth week and the Jewish age has been interrupted. This interval is the church age and was not foreseen in the Old Testament."[3] These statements represent very generally the views held by those whose theology is based upon the Scofield Reference Bible where we

(1) Ironside, Harry A., THE LAMP OF PROPHECY, Page 143
(2) Ironside, Harry A., THE GREAT PARENTHESIS, Page 23
(3) Feinberg, Chas. L., PREMILLENNIALISM AND AMILLENNIALISM, Page 109-111

read, "the church corporately is not in the vision of the Old Testament prophets."[4]

We have already expressed the opinion that this interpretation does an injustice to Scripture, for it is based upon passages which have quite different contextual implications. Dispensationalists contend that the existence of the Christian church had always been a hidden mystery until God revealed it to the apostle Paul. This view is based upon Ephesians 3:1-13 and Colossians 1:23-29. Neither the writer of these Epistles nor the Spirit inspiring him meant that his words should be difficult to understand. There is, therefore, no mystery here that is beyond the average man's comprehension. The apostle Paul is comparing the authority and the genuineness of his apostleship to the Gentiles, with that of his brethren to the circumcision. God had made known to Paul something which previously had not been universally understood — "That the Gentiles should be fellow heirs, and of the same body, and partakers of His promise in Christ by the Gospel" (Ephesians 3:6). It is clear that the Jews did not generally understand that the salvation of the Gentiles was included in the Divine purpose. In fact, the Jews were always reluctant to think of the Gentiles as being of any concern to God. The four-cornered sheet was lowered three times and its accompanying admonition thrice repeated in order to send Peter to the house of Cornelius.

All this does not mean that the church was a mystery first revealed to Paul, as some current writers would have us believe. Naturally they suggest that the surprising rejection of Jesus Christ by the Jews had to unfold another surprise. The Jewish age was interrupted and the church age interjected as the next best expedient. The Gospel of the Kingdom was laid away until "a more convenient season," and "the Gospel of the grace of God began to be preached." One would almost be tempted to label all this as being specially meant for people who are fond of exegetical gymnastics. It is quite plain to

(4) Scofield, C. I., THE SCOFIELD REFERENCE BIBLE, Page 711

the student of Scripture that Paul never claimed to be the
first person to discover the place of the New Testament church
in the Divine purpose. Here are Paul's own words concerning
this matter, "Which in other ages was not made known unto the
sons of men, AS IT IS NOW REVEALED unto His holy
apostles and prophets by the Spirit" (Ephesians 3:5). Paul
does not teach that this matter had always been a hidden
mystery, but simply says that it was not made known to the
same degree. The Old Testament prophecies certainly contain
promises of blessing for the Gentiles. If the church remained
a hidden mystery until its discovery by Paul, one feels like asking
what Jesus Christ meant and what Peter would have understood by the phrase, "Upon this rock I will build my church"
(Matthew 16:18). It is not quite enough for us that the
Scofield Reference Bible has in the preface to Ephesians three,
"The church a mystery hidden from past ages."[5] There ought
to be something stronger and more conclusive than a Scofield
footnote to convince people that the church which Peter knew
and the church which Paul discovered were not the same. The
hair-splitting practice of differentiating between a "body
church" and a "bride church" is surely something that cannot
seem reasonable to most people.

How alien to traditional Christianity is this dividing of the
redeemed of the Lord into different entities known as *body* and
bride, the bride and *the friends of the bridegroom* according
to the period in which they lived, as though salvation were
offered on different terms! This is not rightly dividing the Word
of truth, but wrongly dividing the church of God. It is putting
asunder what God hath joined together.

Let us turn our attention to Acts 3:24 where Peter is explaining miracles wrought by the power of Christ in these
words: "Yea, and all the prophets from Samuel and those that
follow after, as many as have spoken, have likewise foretold
of these days." We also find Peter in his first Epistle writing

_____
(5)   Scofield, C. I., THE SCOFIELD REFERENCE BIBLE, Page 1252

these words: "Receiving the end of your faith, even the salvation of your souls. Of which salvation the prophets have enquired and searched diligently, who prophesied of the grace that should come unto you: Searching what, or what manner of time the Spirit of Christ which was in them did signify, when it testified beforehand the sufferings of Christ, and the glory that should follow. Unto whom it was revealed, that not unto themselves, but unto us they did minister the things, which are now reported unto you by them that have preached the gospel unto you . . ." (I Peter 1:9-12). The dispensationalist tells us that the prophets did not see the church age and that this interval, or parenthesis, was not foreseen in the Old Testament. The Holy Spirit through Peter says that the Old Testament prophets, "prophesied of the grace that should come unto us." The Holy Spirit also says that the Spirit of Christ in the Old Testament prophets testified of "the suffering of Christ and the glory that should follow." This "glory that should follow" the sufferings of Christ must include all that He accomplished by His sufferings. We think "the glory that should follow" must include His resurrection, His ascension and His ultimate return. It also includes Pentecost and all the work accomplished by the Holy Spirit from that day to this. When, therefore, the prophets spoke of the glory that should follow His sufferings, they were referring to some events of the Gospel age. Our Lord gently chided the sorrowing disciples on the Emmaus road for their slowness of heart and inability to understand from the writings of the prophets that Christ should suffer and enter into glory. Surely, then, the prophets had foreseen the church age.

Paul and James, the Lord's brother, quoted the Old Testament prophecies as applying to the New Testament church. If, in the face of these facts, it is still denied that the church is not seen in the Old Testament, it is because apostolic evidence is disregarded.

The major claim of those who represent the dispensational school is that they "take Scripture as its stands" and interpret the Bible literally. One writer says, "No interpretation can be at all satisfactory that does not allow words to have their natural meaning."[6] This does not take into consideration the important fact that we must use natural language to discuss spiritual things. If we cannot give natural language a spiritual meaning, we are left without a medium of expression. Those who boast of being literalists and who describe all others by the reproachful terms of "spiritualizers" are not always too consistent, nor do they themselves practice the method they commend to others. They insist upon the principle of literal interpretation only when it is found useful to maintain a certain point of view. This freedom of interpretation monopolized and claimed by dispensationalists is illustrated by a prominent Canadian radio preacher who says of the book of Revelation, ". . . take it literally. Where the literal sense makes good sense, then why look for any other sense, and where the literal sense makes nonsense, then take it in a figurative sense."[7]

A certain evangelist makes the plea, "Do not explain away the Bible, but take it at face value. God's Word says what it means and means what it says." However, we find on the very next page these words: "The Roman Empire is represented by the legs of iron and feet part of iron, and part of clay. The two legs seem to represent the division of the Roman Empire into the Eastern and the Western, and the toes evidently represent kings or kingdoms which are fragments of the Roman Empire . . . The Roman Empire was not divided into the toes when Christ was here. It is now in the toes age."[8] It is beside our purpose to criticize the interpretation, but we simply point out that even the author does not think that "the Bible says what it means or means what it says."

---

(6) Feinberg, Chas. L., PREMILLENNIALISM AND AMILLENNIALISM, Page 41
(7) Murray, Alexander, RADIO ADDRESSES ON THE BOOK OF REVELATION, Page 5.
(8) Rice, John R., CHRIST'S EARTHLY REIGN, Page 12-13

Dr. Scofield warns us that the expression, "throne of David,"[9] is a phrase as definitely historical as the throne of the Hohenzollerns, and as little admits of spiritualizing. He affirms that the Old Testament prophets had no vision or conception of the church, yet he finds the church typified in the Book of Ruth and the Song of Solomon and so states in his introduction to these books. With the same inconsistency, it is claimed that when God told Abraham that his seed would be as numerous as the dust of the earth, God meant the natural seed of Abraham, but when God said his seed would be as numerous as the stars of heaven, God meant Abraham's spiritual seed. Deuteronomy 1:10, "The Lord your God hath multiplied you, and, behold, ye are this day as the stars of heaven for multitude," does not support this assumption, but rather contradicts it, for Moses is addressing the natural seed in these words. But the Scofield Reference Bible abounds with this sort of typology and yet it is not permissible for anyone else to take the same liberty with the prophecies of the Old Testament that Dr. Scofield takes with its history. Dr. William L. Pettingill says, "Much prophecy remains to be fulfilled, but all fulfilled prophecy has been fulfilled literally."[10] We have to say in all charity that this statement lacks due consideration. Let us go back to Genesis 3:15 and see whether the very first promise of the Redeemer was fulfilled literally. All Christians agree that this promise was fulfilled in Christ, but no one has ever claimed that His heel was literally bruised by a serpent or that He crushed a serpent's head. The twenty-second Psalm is accepted by all Christians as a prophetic description of our Lord's passion, but it was not fulfilled literally. Notice some of its words — "Many bulls have compassed me: strong bulls of Bashan have beset me round . . . For dogs have compassed me . . . Save me from the lion's mouth: for thou hast heard me from the horns of the unicorns." No literalist would contend that this was ever fulfilled "literally," but it was fulfilled

(9) Scofield, C. I., THE SCOFIELD REFERENCE BIBLE, Page 721
(10) Pettingill, W. L., GOD'S PROPHECIES FOR PLAIN PEOPLE, Page 228

none the less. The same principle applies to the works of the prophets. There is no limit to the depths of absurdity to which we shall descend by a literal interpretation. What will the literalist make of Isaiah 7:20, "In the same day will the Lord shave with a razor that is hired"? We do not desire here to be irreverent, but simply to point out the hopelessness of the principle which we are asked to carry into practice. Will the literalist claim that the promises concerning Christ and His forerunner have been fulfilled literally: "Every valley shall be exalted and every mountain and hill shall be made low"? Will he further insist that Christ is a twig or a branch growing out of the stem of Jesse? As a matter of fact, many of the promises which the dispensationalist interprets to predict the restoration of the natural Israel declare that David will be their king, but David is spiritualized to mean Christ while the rest of the passage is usually given a literal interpretation.

We now come to touch upon a question which dispensationalists frequently ask, and which is repeated by Dr. Charles L. Feinberg in a recent work. "Spiritualizers find it hard to explain — and no one has successfully attempted it — why the Scriptures do not mean what they say and why they do not say what they mean? Is it not strange that God who called light into existence with two words should not be able to say what He means?"[11] Our answer is that it is not a question of Divine inability, but of human incapacity. God could say what He means, but men could not understand Him. Christ alluded to this human limitation when He declared that He had many things to tell His disciples, but they could not understand them at that time. This point may be illustrated if we try to imagine how one could have talked to American Indians two or three centuries ago about such inventions as trains, airplanes, automobiles, radios, and telegraphy. These terms would have had no meaning to them; and if they were to have the faintest conception of what was meant, the teacher would have had

(11) Feinberg, Chas. L., PREMILLENNIALISM AND AMILLENNIALISM, Page 41

to employ the words and figures with which they were familiar. It would not necessarily have been a case of inability on the part of the teacher to express his thoughts, but of inability on the part of the people to comprehend. This is the situation confronting us in the Bible. The Old Testament prophets used the figures and circumstances with which people were familiar in order to teach spiritual truths. They addressed a people accustomed to captivity and bondage from the earliest recorded point in their history, a people whose ruling passion was to possess and own their land, and regarded such a possession as the greatest blessing conceivable. It was, therefore, under this figure that the prophets had to describe the new heavens and the new earth. There the inhabitants should live in perfect peace and bliss. When the prophets would teach the eternal abolition of danger and fear from that state of existence it was convenient for them to say, "No lion shall be there, no weapons of war shall be forged for human destruction, and even a little child shall be safe anywhere in the universe." This was the only way in which the Hebrews could understand anything of what God was preparing for His own people.

The Lord Jesus Christ, Himself, followed this method of instruction. In speaking of the new birth, He employed the figures of wind and water. In speaking of the Spirit which His people should receive He spoke of their having a well of water within them. In speaking of their influence in society, He said, "Ye are the salt of the earth. Ye are the light of the world." He spiritualized Old Testament prophecies on various occasions as in Matthew 12:20 and Luke 1:78. In the book of Acts, we find Peter spiritualizing the sixteenth Psalm as foretelling the resurrection of Christ. The apostle Paul, speaking in a Jewish synagogue at Antioch in Pisidia (Acts 13:34), declared that Isaiah's prophecy concerning "the sure mercies of David" (Isaiah 55:3) was a foretelling of the resurrection. James, the Lord's brother, showed that the prophecy of Amos concerning the building of the tabernacle of David and the raising of the ruins thereof, was then being fulfilled in the conversion of the Gentiles to Christianity. All the apostles give spiritual interpretations of the Old Testament prophecies, and literalists do not find fault with them for that. It is universally agreed that the chief cornerstone laid in Zion is to be interpreted as Jesus Christ. Peter likens Christians to living stones built up into a spiritual temple. The apostle Paul, speaking of the experiences of Israel in the wilderness says, "And did all eat the same spiritual meat; and did all drink the same spiritual drink; for they drank of that spiritual Rock that followed them: and that Rock was Christ" (I Corinthians 10:3-4). Here we have a spiritual rock.

Surely there is here a basis of argument and disagreement between dispensationalists and Paul. Much more could be said of his allegorizing of Abraham, Sarah, and Hagar, as representing spiritual realities. Time would fail us to follow this principle through the Epistle to the Hebrews where even Zion and Jerusalem are spiritualized. If the literalist still insists that we are spiritualizing prophecy, we can at least boast of being in very excellent company. The same cannot be said of the literalist. He is following the Jewish method of interpretation which led its exponents to expect a literal fulfillment of every prophecy and which led them to reject and crucify their Messiah. Paul says that this was done "because they knew Him not, nor yet the voices of the prophets which are read every Sabbath day" (Acts 13:27). The plain truth is that there is not one chapter of the prophetic Scriptures which can be taken with absolute literalness and shown to prove the restoration of natural Israel and the establishing of a Palestinian kingdom in which Jews will predominate, with Jerusalem as capital and Christ as king.

We believe, therefore, that the only safe method of interpretation is neither strictly literal, nor strictly spiritual; but that whenever possible the New Testament should be allowed to explain the Old. Augustine, of Hippo, had found the secret of true interpretation and expressed it in these words: "The New was in the Old concealed. The Old is in the New revealed."

Chapter 4.

The Testimony of the Prophets

WE HAVE dealt in the previous chapter with the manner in which Scripture has authorized and exemplified the interpretation of prophecy and with this equipment we proceed to examine the testimony of the prophets relative to our inquiry concerning the restoration of Israel and the re-establishing of the Hebrew economy in the latter days. We remember that our Lord expounded the Scripture, beginning at Moses and all the prophets. In keeping with this pattern, we shall first consider the plain predictions of Moses. It is to be expected that God's inspired prophets will not contradict one another. If Moses, as the Divine spokesman, promised a Jewish restoration, we shall expect the other prophets to do likewise. For indeed, the last of the Old Testament prophets calls upon his contemporaries to remember the law of Moses. If Moses promised a dispersion rather than a restoration, the testimony of the prophets must agree. What, then, did Moses promise to Israel? When he was still leading the people through the desert on the way to Canaan, he revealed in plain, unmistakable terms, the conditions on which they should remain in permanent possession of the land. A rigid monotheism was to be maintained; no other God beside Jehovah was to be worshipped. Fraternization, covenants, and intermarriages with the heathen were strictly forbidden, and absolute obedience to God enjoined as a condition to continual possession of Canaan. The alternative to this was expressed in language truly terrifying. The book of Deuteronomy abounds with warnings of what should happen to the nation in the event of an apostasy; and Moses, foreseeing the apostasy, went so far as to compose a song which the children were to memorize so that when evil should come upon them they should remember that it was a fulfillment of the Divine promise. We suggest that our readers study the twenty-eighth chapter of Deuteronomy, which was so literally fulfilled in the overthrow of Jerusalem and the final dispersion of the Jews in A. D. 70. The predictions of Moses have been corroborated by Joshua who, in his final message to the people whom he had led into Canaan, said: "Therefore it shall come to pass, that as all good things are come upon you, which the Lord your God promised you; so shall the Lord bring upon you all the evil things, until he hath destroyed you from off this good land which the Lord your God hath given you. When ye have transgressed the convenant of the Lord your God, which He commanded you, and have gone and served other gods, and bowed yourselves down to them; then shall the anger of the Lord be kindled against you, and ye shall perish quickly from off the good land which He hath given unto you" (Joshua 23:15-16). The book of Judges bears witness to their tragic breach of covenant with God and to their idolatrous disobedience.

The Davidic covenant, of which much has been said, was to the effect that his seed would sit upon his throne and had its natural fulfillment in the reign of King Solomon. Its eternal aspects include the Lord Jesus Christ of the seed of David; and in the book of Acts, Peter insists that Christ's resurrection and ascension fulfilled God's promise to David that his seed should sit upon his throne. (See Acts 2:30.) Why insist, then, on a literal fulfillment of a promise which the Scriptures certify to have had a spiritual fulfillment? The promise of the Davidic covenant for David's natural seed can be ascertained by reading the words spoken by God to King Solomon, David's son and successor: "But if ye shall at all turn from me, ye or your children, and will not keep my commandments and my statutes which I have set before you, but go and serve other gods, and worship them: Then will I cut off Israel out of the land which I have given them: and this house, which I have hallowed for

My name, will I cast out of my sight; and Israel shall be a proverb and a byword among all people: And at this house, which is high, every one that passeth by it shall be astonished, and shall hiss; and they shall say, Why hath the Lord done thus unto this land, and to this house? And they shall answer, Because they forsook the Lord their God, Who brought forth their fathers out of the land of Egypt, and have taken hold upon other gods, and have worshipped them, and served them: therefore hath the Lord brought upon them all this evil" (I Kings 9:6-9). These words of God have about them a fearful finality which can be ignored only by a dogged determination to maintain a theory, without regard to evidence to the contrary.

We now come to the book of Isaiah which is supposed to contain the fullest account of the earthly kingdom. As we pass through this marvelous book, we cannot but be conscious of a poignant regret that so many of our brethren in the Lord interpret, as applying to an earthly Jewish kingdom of a thousand years' duration, the glorious promises of that everlasting kingdom planned in the eternal councils of God and which shall have its consummation and permanence in the new heavens and the new earth, which Isaiah specifically mentions. In dealing with the works of the prophets, we are never to forget that their utterances may have a dual significance, contemporary and future. Sometimes in the midst of a gloomy description of captivity and sorrow there shines a ray of Messianic hope like the occasional piercing of the clouds by the sun on a stormy day.

Isaiah was a prophet of the southern kingdom of Judah, a contemporary of the prophet Micah. The dominant note in the first part of his message is a denunciation of the nation's wickedness, a prophecy of consequent captivity in Babylon, and of ultimate liberation from that exile. Here and there in the midst of contemporary allusions one finds clear, definite predictions of the Redeemer's advent, notably in the ninth and eleventh chapters. The latter chapter is frequently quoted as descriptive of the earthly kingdom during the millennial reign. This is an effort to make it agree with the doctrine which dispensationalists have built upon the reference to one thousand years in Revelation 20. The eleventh chapter of Isaiah, however, presents under appropriate symbolism the truth of our Lord's first advent, the response of the Gentiles to the Gospel, and the ultimate deliverance of the groaning creation from the curse of sin. It is not a prediction of a millennial kingdom in Palestine. To be sure, the eleventh verse says "the Lord shall set His hand again the second time to recover the remnant of His people," but we have every right to take notice of the kingdoms from which His people are to be gathered — kingdoms which are no longer in existence. At the beginning of the Christian era God did gather a remnant from these lands through the preaching of the Gospel. One writer very eloquently describes the application of this prophecy to the millennium; and writing of Israel's government in that day he says, "The humble of the earth will have their causes adjudicated with uprightness. This will necessitate punishment and even death, which will be speedily meted out."[1] To this agrees another writer who says, "We find that even in that wonderful age there will be the possibility of sickness, but only for any that wilfully disobey the Word of the Lord. Death will no longer be prevalent, but inflicted only judicially."[2] What a millennium! A reign of Christ during which we shall need our hospitals, our jails, our electric chairs, and other means of execution. But let us not lose heart for on the very next page the same writer, quoting Isaiah 25:8, says, "Death is swallowed up in victory and God has wiped away all tears from all faces." We leave it to the reader to judge the incompatibility of these two descriptions by one man. How much better to accept the plain teaching of the Word which says, "When this corruptible shall have put on incorruption, and this mortal shall have put on immortality, then shall be brought to pass the saying that

(1)   Feinberg, Chas. L., PREMILLENNIALISM AND AMILLENNIALISM, Page 57
(2)   Ironside, Harry A., THE LAMP OF PROPHECY, Page 124

is written, Death is swallowed up in victory. O death, where is thy sting? O grave, where is thy victory?" (I Corinthians 15:54-55). This final state is the kingdom of Isaiah's vision. He is naturally referring in many places to his people's return from their captivity in Assyria and in Babylon, but that is the only Jewish restoration of which he speaks. The literalism which would interpret Isaiah's prophecy as applying to an earthly kingdom breaks down upon application. Let the reader examine Isaiah 66:19-23. See the nations from which the people are to be gathered — nations long extinct. Notice the means of transportation; horses, chariots, litters, mules and swift beasts are to be employed. One wonders if the literalist can visualize the returning Jew as rejecting modern means of transportation and reverting to the means and methods used by his ancient ancestors in returning from Babylon. It is to the return from Babylon that the passage refers.

As we come to the prophecy of Jeremiah, we find it expressing the heartfelt sorrow of the patriotic prophet watching his nation on the toboggan slide to captivity and desolation. A nation which has sown the wind must reap the whirlwind. He not only prophesied the captivity, but clearly indicated the length of its duration and instructed the people on how they should react to their captivity. (See Jeremiah 29.) In chapter 30, verses 1-3, the prophet speaks of the return from the exile; and in the following verse his prophetic vision sweeps down the corridors of time and he sees the day of Christ, the Roman conquest and its attendant tribulation, out of which a remnant should be saved to serve the Lord and be the nucleus of the new spiritual Israel. Chapter 31 of this prophecy is frequently quoted in support of the Jewish restoration theory. We have never heard a dispensationalist pointing out that this chapter describes the new covenant and its blessings to the blood-bought church of Christ, the true Israel of God. This was the covenant which our blessed Lord ratified when he said, "This cup is the New Testament in My blood." Jeremiah links up the release of his people from Babylon and the blessings of the gospel, which were still in the distant future. Anyone wishing for assurance about the captivity and restoration to which Jeremiah was referring can turn to the first verse in the book of Ezra and find there the needed information: "Now in the first year of Cyrus, king of Persia, that the Word of the Lord by the mouth of Jeremiah might be fulfilled, the Lord stirred up the spirit of Cyrus, king of Persia, that he made a proclamation throughout all his kingdom . . ." (Ezra 1:1). Ezra seems anxious to tell us that Cyrus's proclamation and Israel's release from Babylon were a fulfillment of Jeremiah's prophecy. How say some among us that this is yet to take place?

The prophecy of Ezekiel is accepted by theologians of all schools as one fraught with difficulties. A student of this book will find it easier to point out the weaknesses of all current theories than to submit a perfect alternative. Dr. Patrick Fairbairn, the distinguished Scottish theologian, when supporting the idea of Jewish restoration, (a position which later he strongly renounced) had this to say of the book of Ezekiel: "I feel constrained to confess myself unable to determine whether it is to be held as properly prophetic or not . . ."[3] When men of such massive intellects find insoluble problems here, it behooves mortals of more limited capacity to proceed with caution. It is quite clear, however, that Ezekiel is a prophet of the captivity. To deal with each part of his prophecy would be a fascinating assignment, but only a brief summary is possible within the scope of this work. The first twenty-four chapters deal with the sinful state of the nation, and predict its downfall. From chapter twenty-five to forty-eight, the book expresses the certainty of a return for the captivity and a rebuilding of the temple with a restoration of the Levitical priesthood and the animal sacrifices. Ezekiel denounces the avarice and the hypocrisy of the shepherds of Israel, promising that God shall raise a good shepherd for the people, a promise

(3) Fairbairn, Patrick, THE PROPHETIC PROSPECTS OF THE JEWS, Page 55

that is fulfilled in Christ as confirmed by the tenth chapter
of John's gospel. The promises of God to gather His people
from all lands, to sprinkle clean water upon them, and to give
them a new heart and a new spirit are manifestly the blessings
of the Covenant of Grace as may be seen from Hebrews
11:16 and 12:22-23. The problem for the dispensationalist is
what to make of "the land." This should not present too great
a difficulty if it be remembered that it is under the figure of a
permanent possession of their land, the prophets describe the
eternal inheritance of the saints. Is it not a sure promise that
in the great day of the Lord, the kingdoms of this world shall
become the kingdom of our God and His Christ? It scarcely
needs to be pointed out that this was the inspired Psalmist's
expectation when he said, "The meek shall inherit the earth."
Our Lord repeated those words in the Sermon on the Mount,
not with reference to Palestine, however, but to the inheritance
of the redeemed.

Ezekiel proceeds to describe the valley of the dry bones
representing the dominion of sin. Then there came the prophetic word followed by the breath from the four winds. Will
anyone deny that this was a vision of the Word made Flesh,
the incarnation of the Son of God, followed in due course by
the descent of the Spirit, coming "with a sound as of a mighty
rushing wind," causing multitudes of men and women to come
from death to life?

The thirty-eighth and thirty-ninth chapters of the book of
Ezekiel present problems of interpretation. It is frequently
found convenient to consign these chapters to the millennial
period and let the matter rest there. That method has for its
proponents the decided advantage of avoiding successful contradiction until the end of the world. In a footnote on chapter
38, Dr. Scofield says, "That the primary reference is to the
northern European powers headed up by Russia all will agree.
The reference to Meshech and Tubal (Moscow and Tobolsk)

is a clear mark of identification."⁴ Dr. Scofield does not tell us
what it is that makes the mark of identification so clear unless
it be that the words begin with the same letters or have the
same root consonants. By this method of interpretation Togar-
mah is said to mean Turkey, while Gomer must mean Germany.
It is all so simple! The Rev. J. M. Kik of Montreal aptly comments on this, saying, "Well, Heaven is not Hell because both
begin with an 'H'."⁵ The truth is that the heathen nations mentioned in these two chapters are also mentioned in the book of
Genesis as the descendants of Japheth and Ham, two sons of
Noah. (See Genesis 10:2.) Some of them are also mentioned in
the book of Revelation in which John identifies them as enemies of God's people. Their final and absolute defeat is
assured. Some of the facts stated concerning them should make
it plain that the prophecy is not to be given a literal interpretation. In Ezekiel, Gog is a leader; in Revelation, a nation.
Dispensationalists have drawn lurid pictures of the battle described in these chapters. The Israelites are said to require
seven months to bury the slain after the battle of Armageddon,
supposedly described here. Of course, the number seven is the
Bible number for completeness. Dr. Patrick Fairbairn points
out some of the difficulties involved in a literal interpretation of
this narrative. He has calculated that if a million men were
employed burying their enemies and each man buried two
people every working day during the 180 working days of the
seven months, they would bury 360,000,000 people. This conservative estimate would be an impossibility in the small land
of Palestine. John, referring in the book of Revelation to the
enemies of the church says, "The number thereof is as the sands
of the sea." These enemies have been active ever since the fall
of man, but their antagonism will come to an end with a final
conflict which Christ shall terminate at His coming.

The eight closing chapters of Ezekiel present difficulties for
all students of the Bible. The Scofield Reference Bible has

(4)   Scofield, C. I., THE SCOFIELD REFERENCE BIBLE, Page 883
(5)   Kik, J. M., BIBLE CHRISTIANITY, Vol. 7, No. 11

but one brief comment on the eight chapters. It places them all in the millennial period and explains the nature of the sacrifices prescribed. Ezekiel is speaking in the twenty-fifth year of the captivity, which was to last seventy years. He is given a vision of the temple which the returning exiles are commanded to build, and instructions concerning the division of the land among the tribes. Here also, one finds a restoration of the Levitical system with all its sacrifices and its special priesthood. Dispensationalists hold that during the millennial period the temple will be rebuilt at Jerusalem and the sacrifices restored. Dr. Scofield says, "Doubtless these offerings will be memorial, looking back to the cross."[6] There is not the slightest allusion to this in Ezekiel. The sacrifices are given their customary and traditional significance. The whole problem is one which dispensationalists prefer to treat with silence. The temple which originally took half a century to build is going to be built in the three and one half years constituting the first half of the great tribulation period. This difficulty is overcome by one dispensationalist who suggests that the Mosque of Omar in Jerusalem can easily be turned into a Jewish temple. The Levitical priesthood which, according to Hebrews 7:11 was eternally abolished and supplanted by the universal priesthood of believers, will be restored during the millennial reign. The things which Paul stigmatized as "beggarly elements" will be instituted as Christian practices during the visible reign of Him Who abolished them forever. The apostle Paul, writing to the Galatians, emphatically declared, "If ye be circumcised, Christ shall profit you nothing" (Galatians 5:2). The continuance of such practices as the ceremonial law required was to Paul the badge of bondage, yet today we are told that these shall be reinstituted during the millennial reign of Christ. In addition to all this, specific directions are given for the marriage of priests, which could hardly apply to any of the saints in the millennial kingdom, since Jesus told us that "in the

(6) Scofield, C. I., THE SCOFIELD REFERENCE BIBLE, Page 890

resurrection they neither marry nor are given in marriage, but are as the angels of God" (Matthew 22:30). Let the reader study these chapters of Ezekiel describing a recrudescence of Mosaic shadows and ceremonial sacrifices, divers washings and rituals, which were abolished by the coming of Him Whom they typified, and imagine their restoration and observance by the people of God once again. It is enough to fill the Christian's heart with revulsion. The veil which was rent at the time of the crucifixion would become intact. Only the high priest could enter in within the veil, and that, after he had offered sacrifice for his own sins and the sins of the people. The Passover, which was abolished by Calvary, would once again take the place of the Lord's Supper. The presence of God would be confined to one spot, and only on that spot could He be worshipped. Our Lord's words to the woman of Samaria would be meaningless: "Jesus saith unto her, Woman, believe me, the hour cometh, when ye shall neither in this mountain, nor yet at Jerusalem, worship the Father . . . God is a Spirit: and they that worship Him must worship Him in Spirit and in truth" (John 4:21, 24). According to dispensationalism, the time shall come when men will have to go to Jerusalem in order to worship God. One writer has estimated the present number of earth's inhabitants as one and a half billion. If transportation could be furnished for them, and it were made possible and mandatory to worship at one shrine at the rate of one hundred thousand a day, only once in forty-two years could the individual draw nigh unto God. The whole idea cannot but be shocking to those who try to visualize its consummation. Dr. Patrick Fairbairn says of the advocates of this theory: "The anomalous position which they occupy cannot possibly last. Consistency will oblige them either to abandon their Judaism or to renounce their evangelism."[7] We cannot believe that such an interpretation of Scripture is glorifying to Him Who is "the end of the law unto righteousness unto them

(7)   Fairbairn, Patrick, THE PROPHETIC PROSPECTS OF THE JEWS, Page 118

that believe," and Who took away "the hand writing of ordinances written against us . . . nailing it to His cross" (Colossians 2:14).

What, then, can these chapters mean? We believe that they mean and express a Divine plan which not only takes in the post-exilic temple, but also reaches forward in vision to that great city of John's vision, the New Jerusalem, with the difference that in John's Holy City there is no temple, for there Jehovah is dwelling in the midst of His people. The Hebrews returning from the captivity did build a temple, but it did not conform to the Divine pattern, for the spiritual and moral defects of the people made that an impossible and unrealized ideal. Here we have the words of God to the prophet: "Thou son of man, show the house to the house of Israel, that they may be ashamed of their iniquities: and let them measure the pattern. And if they be ashamed of all that they have done, show them the form of the house and fashion thereof . . ." (Ezekiel 43:10). God showed them the pattern, but that pattern could not be realized by the earthly Israel, but shall be attained by their spiritual successors. To this ultimate realization the prophecy leads. The forty-seventh chapter refers to a river of living water flowing out from the temple and healing every spot of the universe that it touches. This reminds us that our blessed Lord, under the figure of water, described the Spirit, which those believing on Him should receive. The disciples in the temple of Jerusalem centuries later received that Spirit and from them the Gospel has flowed out to us, and in it we have received an earnest of that inheritance incorruptible, undefiled, and that fadeth not away, reserved in heaven for us.

The prophecy of Zechariah, like that of Ezekiel, lends itself to dispensational interpretations. We take his prophecy as being typical of the works of the so-called Minor Prophets. He was a prophet of the captivity and a considerable portion of his prophecy applies to the people of his day. He who would understand Zechariah must keep in view the whole spiritual panorama from the Babylonian captivity until the establishing of the kingdom of God in all its fulness and glorious consummation. A favorite phrase with Zechariah is "that day," by which is meant the gospel age. The Scofield Reference Bible states that only in Zechariah 9:9 is the gospel age foreseen by the prophet. The passage says, "Rejoice greatly, O daughter of Zion; shout, O daughter of Jerusalem: behold, thy King cometh unto thee: He is just, and having salvation; lowly, and riding upon an ass, and upon a colt the foal of an ass." This verse is referred to by each of the gospel writers as having its fulfillment when Jesus Christ entered Jerusalem for the last time. While that evidence is available, one writer still insists that it will be completely fulfilled only when Christ comes again. We believe that this view is shared by other dispensationalists. With reference to the statement that this is the only verse of the prophecy referring to the gospel age, this can easily be refuted by turning to Zechariah 13:7: "Awake, O sword, against my shepherd, and against the man that is my fellow, saith the Lord of hosts: smite the shepherd, and the sheep shall be scattered: and I will return mine hand upon the little ones . . ." Our blessed Lord quoted this verse as applying to Himself, as we can see by turning to Matthew 26:31 or Mark 14:27. (In this matter, the Scofield Reference Bible contradicts itself, for it has a marginal note opposite John 19:37 showing it to be a fulfillment of Zechariah 12:10).[8]

Time and space will permit but a brief reference here to the passages in Zechariah which are most frequently quoted in support of dispensationalism. In chapter 12:10-14, we read the words: "And I will pour upon the house of David, and upon the inhabitants of Jerusalem, the spirit of grace and supplications; and they shall look upon me whom they have pierced, and they shall mourn for Him, as one mourneth for his only son, and shall be in bitterness for him, as one that is

---

(8) Scofield, C. I., THE SCOFIELD REFERENCE BIBLE, Page 1143

in bitterness for his firstborn. In that day shall there be a great mourning in Jerusalem . . . And the land shall mourn, every family apart . . ." We have before us the records of "that day" (the Gospel dispensation) which the prophet visualizes, although the events are not stated in chronological order. Believing that the best expositor of Scripture is the Bible itself, we turn once more to the New Testament for an explanation of this prophecy. The nineteenth chapter of John's Gospel tells us of certain Old Testament passages which were fulfilled at Calvary: "These things were done, that the Scripture should be fulfilled, A bone of Him shall not be broken. And again another Scripture saith, They shall look on Him whom they pierced" (John 19:36-37). Dispensationalism separates these two passages which the Holy Spirit has brought together, and says one of them is to be fulfilled at the Lord's return. If the pen of inspiration reports that the prophecy has already been fulfilled, we are content to rest our case there.

After the piercing of the Holy One there followed the outpouring of the Spirit and "a great mourning in Jerusalem." As we look back upon Pentecost, there is no difficulty in seeing where and when this phase of the prophecy was fulfilled. "The spirit of grace and supplication" was poured out on that day, and there was certainly a great mourning in Jerusalem. It is scarcely possible for us to imagine the spectacle of thousands of men crushed by genuine repentance "pricked in their hearts" with a conviction of sin and crying out, "Men and brethren what shall we do?" The mourning was individual and personal, as described in Zechariah 12:11-14.

The thirteenth chapter of Zechariah also refers to the opening of the fountain which was to take away sin and uncleanness from the house of David and the inhabitants of Jerusalem, which will result in cutting off the names of the idols out of the land. In the sixth verse of this chapter we read: "And one shall say unto Him, What are these wounds in Thy hands? Then He shall answer, Those with which I was wounded in the house of My friends." We have already stated that the seventh verse, "Awake, O sword, against my shepherd," was fulfilled on the night of our Lord's arrest in the Garden of Gethsemane, and we have this on our Lord's own authority. We believe that both verses allude to the same occasion. It is altogether inconceivable to us that at our Lord's return, Jews from all parts of the world will look upon Him Whom they have pierced and will be saved by sight, as dispensationalists suggest will be the case. We do not find any authority in the Word of God leading us to believe that salvation will ever be offered to a lost sinner other than by faith in Jesus Christ. "We walk not by sight, but by faith."

Zechariah fourteen sums up briefly the gospel age, although not strictly in chronological order. The destruction of Jerusalem is here described as being closely connected with the planting of our Lord's feet upon the Mount of Olives. We do not think that too much emphasis should be given to the supposed geological fault running through the Mount of Olives as indicating its readiness to fall apart when it shall be touched by the feet of our returning Lord. The same geological fault can be found in any part of the surrounding territory. The Lord Jesus Christ has already stood upon the Mount of Olives, and from its brow He looked down upon the city which represented the Hebrew nation. That nation fell into two parts at His coming, and those two parts have been separated ever since "by a very great valley," an impassable gulf. Especially was this true at the destruction of Jerusalem, when the separation of the two elements became complete and absolute. This was in keeping with His own words in Luke 12:51-53: "Suppose ye that I am come to give peace on earth? I tell you, Nay; but rather division: For from henceforth there shall be five in one house divided, three against two, and two against three. The father shall be divided against the son, and the son against the father; the mother against the daughter, and the daughter against the mother; the mother-in-law against her daughter-in-law, and the daughter-in-law against her mother-in-law."

The remainder of chapter fourteen describes living waters going out from Jerusalem, the gospel of salvation bringing men under the sovereign sway of Jesus Christ. How very inadequate and carnal it is to think of this as a river bringing fertility and prosperity to the land and replenishing the Dead Sea with all manner of fish by reason of the healing virtues of the water! The only living waters recognized by the New Testament proceed from the throne of God and the Lamb. Verses eight to ten of this fourteenth chapter reveal the final consummation of the Divine plan when God shall have made all things new, and when "holiness unto the Lord" shall characterize every creature and every object in God's new world.

We bring this chapter to a close, wishing that space and time had permitted a fuller treatment of the ground covered. In closing, we submit to our readers a proposition which we do not think anyone can deny or disprove. Every promise which dispensationalists interpret as supporting a Jewish restoration is a promise given either before or during the time of Israel's captivity in Babylon, and refers either to that captivity and restoration or, under appropriate figures and symbols, to the gospel era, or to the ultimate setting up of that everlasting kingdom, which shall never be destroyed, which is neither Palestinian nor political, and whose citizens shall be neither Jews nor Gentiles, but new creatures in Christ Jesus. It is Christ, rather than the Hebrew people, Who is the subject of the Old Testament prophets. The Bible announces no special plan of salvation for the Jews in this present age. To be sure, the nation was sovereignly chosen by God as the channel through which His oracles might be given to the world; but God no longer deals with them as a chosen nation, but as individual sinners to whom He offers salvation by Jesus Christ.

Chapter 5.

The Testimony of Jesus

THE very title of this chapter is a reminder of the words of Scripture telling us that "the testimony of Jesus is the Spirit of Prophecy." He is to the Old Testament prophecies what the Spirit is to the body. Without Him prophecy is lifeless. The student of Scripture is constantly amazed to find how the entire program of Christ's earthly life had been carefully planned from all eternity and carried out to the letter when the "fulness of the time had come." The New Testament relates one incident after another in Christ's life and tells us that this came to pass "that the Scriptures might be fulfilled." He, Himself, frequently quoted the prophetic Scriptures, saying, "This that is written of Me must be fulfilled." His birth and birthplace, His mission and rejection, the piercing of His hands and feet, His dying thirst, and even the disposal of His garments were parts of an eternal plan revealed by God to his servants, the prophets.

Many of us have been taught from childhood that our Lord Jesus Christ came into this world "to give His life a ransom for many." This belief is quite in keeping with His words contained in the Scriptures of the New Testament, and is the age-old heritage of the Christian church. A new thing under the sun has been discovered in the realm of theology during this last century. Like many other grievous heresies it began with zealous and sincere Christian people. It proceeded cautiously at first, but now is being preached, taught, printed, and published; and worse still, it is being accepted by many of the Lord's own people because of their confidence in those engaged in its propagation. It has been our great privilege for many years to enjoy the Christian fellowship of dispensationalists in Presbyterian, Baptist, Congregational and other churches, as well as in the assemblies of so-called Plymouth Brethren. We have found them to be Christians of the highest type, men and women who love the Lord. We therefore question if any great numbers of those Christians realize that the dispensationalism to which they are committed, followed to its logical conclusion, denies that the cross was a part of God's original plan. They would be horrified at the very suggestion, as we know too well from our acquaintance with them.

The Palestinian Kingdom theory has become, however, such an obsession with some that it is now claimed that Jesus Christ came into this world primarily for the purpose of setting up the kingdom and being its king. It is contended that the Sermon on the Mount was meant to be the constitution of this kingdom, but the Jews rejected the constitution and therefore the offer of the kingdom was withdrawn and, according to dispensationalism, Christ will have to set it up again at His second coming. It is only then that much of Matthew's Gospel, including the entire Sermon on the Mount, will be applicable. In our day it remains obsolete. One of America's outstanding dispensationalists writes, "We confess very frankly that there are things in the Sermon on the Mount which we do not consider as we seek to order our life, even though we are earnestly trying to order all things after the Word of God. The reason we discard such commands is the same reason for which we do not get a lamb and have it killed on an altar by a priest."[1] Does this mean that the Lord's Prayer, the Golden Rule, and all the moral directives which our Lord gave to His disciples in the fifth, sixth, and seventh chapters of Matthew's gospel are out of place in the Christian church and are not applicable to Christians in any way? Indeed, one writer has gone so far as to state that the Lord's Prayer is as much out of place in the Christian church as the Levitical sacrifices. It is pertinent at this point to inquire when the Lord's Prayer shall be proper and timely. If, as the dispensationalist says, the Sermon on

(1) Barnhouse, D. G., HE CAME TO HIS OWN: BUT, Page 38

the Mount, including the Lord's Prayer, is the constitution of the millennial kingdom it will seem necessary to delete its second petition. Why shall it be necessary to pray "Thy kingdom come" in the millennium when, according to dispensationalism, the kingdom has already been set up? Another writer already referred to speaks of the obsolescence of the ceremonial law of the Old Testament and says, "In precisely the same way we are free from certain passages in the Sermon on the Mount, because the day of their application has not yet come."[2] This interpretation should prove rather convenient to many professing Christians in our day. If the Sermon on the Mount with its moral obligations was meant only for the Jews, this would imply that Christians must look for directions from some other source for the regulation of their conduct. Another writer urges, "Don't go back to the Gospel to find your rule of life; go to the Epistles, because there you have life in the energy of the Holy Spirit. Don't ignore the express will of the Lord."[3] This would seem to suggest that the will of the Lord is found in the Epistles rather than in the Gospels. It would seem to suggest that Paul is to be given precedence over the Master Whom he delighted to serve, and this notwithstanding Jesus' words, "Learn of Me." The explanation of all this can be found in the Scofield Reference Bible, where we read, "The doctrines of grace are to be sought in the Epistles, not in the Gospels." The same writer warns us that, "In approaching the study of the Gospels the mind should be freed, so far as possible, from mere theological conceptions and presuppositions. Especially is it necessary to exclude the notion (a legacy in Protestant thought from post-apostolic and Roman Catholic theology) that the church is the true Israel, and that the Old Testament foreview of the kingdom is fulfilled in the church."[4] Thus we are told to free the mind from what has been admittedly the legacy of the church from post-apostolic times, and be ready to receive

---

(2) Barnhouse, D. G., HE CAME TO HIS OWN : BUT, Page 38
(3) Ironside, Harry A., THE LAMP OF PROPHECY, Page 67
(4) Scofield, C. I., THE SCOFIELD REFERENCE BIBLE, Page 989

that which has been foreign to both apostolic and post-apostolic Christianity. In addition, it is suggested that this savors of Roman Catholic theology in order to prepare and prejudice the unwary into believing that Matthew's Gospel does not apply to our age.

We recall having read a story of a young lad who came in from school with his clothing torn, his general appearance disheveled, and his nose bleeding. He explained that he had been in a fight, which, like every fight in which a boy has taken part, was started by the other fellow. His mother gave him a little lecture on the rewards and the blessedness of the peacemakers, reminding him of the exhortation of Scripture, "To turn the other cheek." To this the lad promptly responded, "Mother, that is from Matthew's Gospel and is meant only for the Jews." This is exactly what is being taught today in many quarters, and it is not possible for us to say how far it is influencing the lives of those whose Christian knowledge is but superficial and whose piety is sufficiently shallow to take advantage of any way of escape from duty or restraint.

It is not, however, the matter of Christian conduct alone that is here involved. The honor of the Lord Jesus Christ is impugned, as is the truth of Scripture and the plan of salvation. The claim of modern dispensationalism is that Jesus Christ came to establish a Jewish kingdom upon the earth; that He offered this kingdom to the Jews, who rejected it; and that this was the kingdom to which John the Baptist and Jesus Christ referred when they said, "The kingdom of heaven is at hand." All this would mean that our blessed Lord came from heaven primarily on a special mission to the Jews. This is exactly what we read in the Scofield Reference Bible which says, "The mission of Jesus was primarily to the Jew. He was made under the law and was minister of the circumcision for the truth of God."[5] The mission to the Jews which is emphasized is the offer of a political kingdom which they, how-

---

(5) Scofield, C. I., THE SCOFIELD REFERENCE BIBLE, Page 989

ever, rejected, making necessary the death of Christ on the cross. Thus atonement was made for the sins of the world only because the original plan miscarried.

We have already suggested that the honor of the Lord Jesus is here impugned, and we now cite the facts. It is a matter of record that when the Jews wished to bring about the death of Jesus of Nazareth, they found it necessary to concoct charges that would be calculated to interest the Roman governor whose prerogative it was to pronounce and carry out the death sentence. Pilate was not interested in the accusations of blasphemy which the Jews sought to substantiate by false witnesses. Pilate did not care whether or not Jesus claimed to be the Son of God, a claim which greatly stirred the members of the Sanhedrin. If the Jews were to get Pilate's ear, the charge against Jesus had to be political rather than religious. He had to be accused of a capital crime deserving of death. What more fitting offense than sedition! This was quickly decided upon and the writers of the third and fourth Gospels vividly describe the charges. Luke says, ". . . the whole multitude of them arose, and led Him to Pilate. And began to accuse Him saying, We found this fellow perverting the nation, and forbidding to give tribute to Caesar, saying He Himself is Christ a King" (Luke 23:1, 2). Pilate, having heard the name of Caesar brought into the proceedings, was duty bound to make an investigation. He faced Jesus with the question: "Art thou the King of the Jews? . . . Jesus answered, My kingdom is not of this world: if My kingdom were of this world, then would My servants fight, that I should not be delivered to the Jews: but now is My kingdom not from hence" (John 18:33, 36). This seems rather conclusive. It was sufficient to convince Pilate that the charge of sedition had no basis in fact. He, therefore, promptly reported to the priests who waited outside the judgment hall, "I find no fault in this man." The fact that Pilate had satisfied himself concerning the political innocence of Jesus meant nothing to the Jews. We read that when they heard this, ". . . they were the more fierce, saying, He stirreth up the people, teaching throughout all Jewry, beginning from Galilee to this place" (Luke 23:5). As soon as Pilate heard that Galilee was involved he had Jesus sent to Herod, the puppet king whose jurisdiction included Galilee, and who would tolerate no usurper within his domains. It was Herod's duty to himself and to the Roman power which he represented to ascertain whether or not Jesus of Nazareth had political ambitions which might endanger the existing regime. Herod, having examined Jesus, sent Him back to Pilate, who reported the result of the joint investigation in these words: "Ye have brought this man unto me, as one that perverteth the people: and, behold, I, having examined Him before you, have found no fault in this man touching those things whereof ye accuse Him: No, nor yet Herod: for I sent you to him; and, lo, nothing worthy of death is done unto Him. I will therefore chastise Him, and release Him" (Luke 23:14-16).

There, then, is the record. The two people whose lives and interests were most vitally affected both absolved Jesus Christ of the charge of offering national independence to the Jews and offering Himself as king. The custom of the times demanded that the criminal's accusation be nailed above his head on the cross. Pilate therefore wrote the title, "Jesus of Nazareth, the king of the Jews" (John 19:19). "Then said the chief priests of the Jews to Pilate, Write not, the King of the Jews: but that He said, I am King of the Jews. Pilate answered,What I have written I have written" (John 19:21-22). Thus it would seem as though God Himself sovereignly prohibited and prevented any suggestion that Jesus Christ laid claim to an earthly kingdom of the Jews. He is King of a kingdom in which there is neither Jew nor Greek, Barbarian, Scythian, bond nor free. We cannot refrain from interjecting here the observation that in our acquaintance with ecclesiastical and doctrinal history we have never found any instance where the accusations of the Jews against Jesus were being upheld by the Christian church until the rise of modern dispensationalism.

We have pointed out that the truth of God was also impugned here. By the truth of God we mean the Scriptures of the Old and New Testaments. The great majority of Christians believe that the sacrifices and ceremonial requirements of the Old Testament ritual were foreshadowings of the greater and all-sufficient sacrifice offered on Calvary. When Abraham with his son was climbing Mount Moriah to worship God, Isaac asked, "Where is the lamb?" That question came reverberating down the corridors of time. Abraham gave it an inspiring and prophetic answer: ". . God will provide Himself a lamb" (Genesis 22:8). This was Abraham's answer to his son and also God's promise to the fallen sons of Adam, who like Micah, were asking, "Wherewith shall I come before the Lord?" (Micah 6:6). The prophets, each in his day, anticipated the coming of One Who should make His soul an offering for sin. The centuries passed on and God's hour was drawing nigh. A God-fearing young man in Judea contemplating marriage with a chaste young woman found her to be with child. His natural fears and consternation were quickly allayed by an angel who informed him that his wife, Mary, should bring forth a child begotten of the Holy Ghost, and added, ". . thou shalt call His name Jesus: for He shall save His people from their sins" (Matthew 1:21). This announcement contained no hint of an earthly kingdom. When eventually the birth of Jesus was announced by the heavenly choir to the shepherds on the plains of Bethlehem the words of that announcement were, "Fear not: for, behold, I bring you good tidings of great joy, which shall be to all people. For unto you is born this day in the city of David a Saviour, which is Christ the Lord" (Luke 2:10, 11). The dominant note in their heavenly announcement was that God had provided and sent a Saviour to a lost world. Considerable prominence has been given to the words of the angel Gabriel to the mother of Jesus, promising that "the Lord God shall give Him the throne of his father David: and he shall reign over the house of Jacob forever and of His Kingdom there shall be no end" (Luke 1:32-33). The reference to His possession of the throne of his father David has been interpreted as a positive proof that Christ shall be seated on David's original throne in Jerusalem. If we believe in the inspiration of Scripture, this is adequately explained in Acts 2:30 which says of David, "Therefore being a prophet, and knowing that God had sworn with an oath to him, that of the fruit of his loins, according to the flesh, he would raise up Christ to sit on his throne." Peter says this promise had its fulfillment in Christ's resurrection. The statement that "He shall reign over the house of Jacob forever" surely signifies the eternal nature of his kingdom, and is sufficient proof that the kingdom is not Palestinian. When Mary and Joseph presented their child in the temple, fulfilling the requirements of the law, the aged Spirit-filled Simeon praised God for this "light to lighten the Gentiles, and the glory of Thy people Israel" (Luke 2:32). Simeon had been waiting for the consolation of Israel and was now content to depart, for his eyes had seen His salvation. (See Luke 2:25-30.) In that same breath he warned Mary that a sword should pass through her soul. There was no word of an earthly kingdom there.

Thirty years later, John the Baptist, the great forerunner, preached in the wilderness of Judea, commanding the people to repent and flee from the wrath to come, warning them that the kingdom of heaven was at hand. This kingdom of heaven, literally "the kingdom of the heavens," has always been interpreted by the Christian church as a kingdom of unearthly character, spiritual and heavenly rather than earthly in its features. Dispensationalism, however, insists that this means a literal kingdom to be established in Palestine, of which Christ shall be literally the king. But we must ask whether John the Baptist so understood his own pronouncements. He described himself as "The voice of one crying in the wilderness, Prepare ye the way of the Lord" (Matthew 3:3). This coming Lord was greater than he. He had his fan in His hand and would thoroughly purge His floor gathering the wheat into His garner and burning the chaff with unquenchable fire. He would baptize, not with water, but with the Holy Ghost and with fire. Who would understand such words to be descriptive of the function of an earthly king? But John does not leave us in doubt as to what he thinks of Jesus Christ, for one day as he preached on the banks of the Jordan and saw Jesus, he cried, "Behold the Lamb of God which taketh away the sin of the world" (John 1:29). The age-old question had been, "Where is the Lamb?" The exhilarating and gratifying answer was, "Behold the Lamb." What an unexpected comment on this text we have found in a book by a leading dispensationalist! On one page he draws our attention to the fact that John the Baptist was filled with the Holy Ghost from his mother's womb; but on another page we read these words, "John spoke of Christ as Saviour only in one passage and that on the day of the baptism of the Lord, and most significantly it is only in the fourth Gospel that it is recorded. It can also be demonstrated that John the Baptist did not understand what he was saying when he cried, 'Behold the Lamb of God Who taketh away the sin of the world,' and later when he was in prison he sent disciples to ask the Lord if He, Jesus, was really the One Who should come, or if another were to be expected."[6] Here, then, we find an attempt to maintain a theory, for which any liberal theologian would be loudly criticized, but which dispensationalism, "rightly dividing the word of truth," can manipulate to suit its purpose. It is pointed out that this occurs in but one passage, "and most significantly in the fourth Gospel." Surely this fact does not deprive it of its force and veracity. If we adopt this rule of exegesis it will apply also to John 3:16, and to John 14, as well as to the great *Logos* passages in the prologue to the fourth Gospel. Dispensationalism's millennium is based upon a statement which occurs only once, and that in a highly symbolical book. The application of the same rule would

---

(6) Barnhouse, D. G., HE CAME TO HIS OWN: BUT, Page 19

certainly establish the same conclusion, and that is that it does not mean what it says.

Another writer reaffirms "dispensational truth" in a little book containing a chapter dealing with the question, "Was the Kingdom Offered Israel and Rejected?"[7] The writer appears to be in difficulty as he tries to evade the logical conclusion of his own statements. In his attempt to prove that Christ offered the Jews a kingdom he does not quote the words of Jesus Himself, but gives an exposition of the second Psalm. This sort of reasoning cannot be very satisfactory to those well acquainted with the Word of God. But the author in his preface suggests that we search "the Word of God to see if these things be so." This search will not fail to elucidate the meaning of the second Psalm. The book of Acts tells us that the apostles regarded this Psalm as having its fulfillment in the attitude of Herod and Pontius Pilate toward Jesus Christ. When the apostles had been threatened by the Sanhedrin and reported that matter to their fellow Christians we read that, "When they heard that, they lifted up their voice to God with one accord, and said, Lord, thou art God, which has made heaven, and earth, and the sea, and all that in them is: Who by the mouth of Thy servant David hast said, Why did the heathen rage, and the people imagine vain things? The kings of the earth stood up, and the rulers were gathered together against the Lord, and against His Christ. For of a truth against Thy holy child Jesus, Whom thou hast anointed, both Herod and Pontius Pilate, with the Gentiles, and the people of Israel, were gathered together, For to do whatsoever Thy hand and Thy counsel determined before to be done" (Acts 4:24-28). Thus in the antagonism of the rulers to Jesus Christ, and in their continued opposition to the Gospel after Pentecost, the inspired apostles of Christ found a fulfillment of the second Psalm. Surely we are on solid ground here. We know that the second Psalm is prophetic of a well-nigh universal opposition to Christ which is to characterize the

---

(7)   Ironside, Harry A., THE LAMP OF PROPHECY, Page 55

Gospel age from beginning to end. To all this the Divine response is, "Yet have I set My king upon My holy hill of Zion" (Psalm 2:6). Observe it does not say "I will," but "I have."

We now turn to the words of Jesus Himself, to see if they suggest the offering of an earthly kingdom. One of His earliest recorded conversations was with a master in Israel who was interested in the kingdom. Jesus immediately told him that this kingdom could be entered only by a spiritual birth. Nicodemus could not understand, and Jesus had to describe the new birth under the figures of wind and water; but even then he asked, "How can these things be?" Jesus continued to emphasize the spiritual nature of the kingdom; but recognizing the natural man's difficulty in apprehending spiritual truth He said, "If I have told you earthly things, and ye believe not, how shall ye believe, if I tell you of heavenly things?" (John 3:12). This great third chapter of John universally recognized as the heart of the gospel, seems to emphasize the word "whosoever." It is, therefore, not a kingdom for Jews, but a kingdom for all who are willing to enter into it. It is quite correct to say that the Jews expected a kingdom of God and of the Jews. It was the very fact that Jesus did not establish such a kingdom which disappointed them so much that they sought to put Him to death. The truth is that instead of offering the Jews an earthly kingdom, the Jews offered the kingdom to Jesus. When He fed the five thousand they were ready to crown Him King, but He rejected the offer: "When Jesus therefore perceived that they would come and take Him by force, to make Him a king, He departed again into a mountain Himself alone" (John 6:15). They would also have crowned Him king just one week before they crucified Him. Their cry to Him as He entered Jerusalem for the last time was "Hosanna" which means "Save us now." The "saving" they wanted was deliverance from their Roman oppressors, whereas the salvation which He came to offer was salvation from sin. The kingdom He came to offer was not of this world and, therefore, contrary to all their dreams and expectations. Was it not the mistake of the Jews down through their long and checkered history that they desired a king like all the nations round about them, thus rejecting the kingdom of God? This is the kingship of which Jesus spoke when He discussed the kingdom of heaven or the kingdom of God. It is obvious that He and the unregenerate Jews never meant the same thing by these terms. Their inability to understand His deeply spiritual teachings made it necessary for Him to teach by parables, a method which was not necessary for Him to use with those who had become enlightened and unto whom "It is given to know the mysteries of the kingdom of God . . ." (Luke 8.10).

It now remains for us to point out where dispensationalism leads those who follow it to its logical conclusions. Its claim that Christ's mission was primarily to offer a kingdom to the Jews, must inevitably relegate the transaction of Calvary to a secondary place in the Divine purpose. The men who advocate "The Kingdom Postponement Theory" have doubtlessly anticipated some of the questions which this theory is bound to raise. One such question is, How could atonement be made for the sins of the world if the Jews had accepted the kingdom and Christ had not died? A leading exponent of this theory says, "In the Gospels the Lord proclaims the Gospel of the kingdom. After the church is taken out, the Gospel of the Kingdom will again be proclaimed, i. e., the Gospel that the king is coming to reign. Now the good news is that God is offering remission of sins."[8] Another advocate of "The Kingdom Postponement Theory" says, "It is idle to speculate on what would happen had the Pharisees and the leaders accepted Jesus as the Messiah and bowed to his standards. Whether he could have found some other way of imputing righteousness to their account is not a question worthy of our discussion."[9] We know

---

(8) Ironside, Harry A., THE LAMP OF PROPHECY, Page 62
(9) Barnhouse, D. G., HE CAME TO HIS OWN: BUT, Page 35

that hypothetical questions have no place where the omniscient God is concerned. But dispensationalism suggests that God had intended to do something and was frustrated by men who were capable of doing so. Inasmuch as the responsibility has been placed in the hands of men it is pertinent to ask, What if those men had made the other choice and accepted the kingdom? S. D. Gordon in his book *Quiet Talks about Jesus* admits this question as pertinent, and endeavors to answer it. It is conceivable that men of his own school would have preferred that Mr. Gordon had not followed this matter to its logical and inevitable conclusion. In doing so he has displayed a measure of courage, if not of orthodoxy. He has dared to say what others have obscurely suggested, but held back because "they feared the people." Mr. Gordon says of the death of Christ, "It can be said at once that His dying was not God's own plan. It was conceived somewhere else and yielded to by God. God had a plan of atonement by which men who were willing could be saved from sin and its effects."[10] We are left in no uncertainty as to what was the original plan of atonement. He asserts that animal sacrifices would accomplish this purpose. Other dispensationalists have not gone as far as Mr. Gordon has in this respect, but we have heard no widespread denial of his views by those who share his dispensationalism.

It gives us no pleasure, but rather sorrow, to make these observations; but we feel that a devotion to Christ and His truth must take precedence over our deference to our fellow man, however highly regarded by ourselves and others.

There was but one kingdom offered by our Lord Jesus Christ. He offers that kingdom to all who will enter into it today. When we accept Him as Saviour and Lord, we have an earnest of that kingdom which is yet to be ours in all its fulness, "an inheritance incorruptible, and undefiled, and that fadeth not

(10) Gordon, S. D., QUIET TALKS ABOUT JESUS, Page 114

away, reserved in heaven for you" (I Peter 1:4). "In heaven" is not the same as "in Palestine." He did not promise a kingdom in which Jews will predominate. The citizens of His kingdom constitute "a chosen generation, a royal priesthood, an holy nation, a purchased people" (I Peter 2:9). Gentile or Jewish origin will make no difference, but a new creation. When He comes again He will call His people to Himself to "inherit the kingdom prepared for you from the foundations of the world" (Matthew 25:34). That kingdom will not be Palestine, any more than it will be Poland. The fact that Jesus did not speak of an earthly, but of a heavenly, not of a material, but of a spiritual kingdom, should be accepted as sufficient proof that it was that spiritual kingdom which was visualized by the prophets. "The testimony of Jesus is the spirit of prophecy."

We cannot think of any proof that should be more conclusive in this respect than the silence of the New Testament regarding any such kingdom. The whole thought is foreign to the revelation given by Jesus Christ.

Chapter 6.

The Teachings of the Apostles

THE apostles who wrote the Epistles of the New Testament had a decided advantage in their possession of certain necessary qualifications. They were all of Hebrew descent and from childhood were familiar with the words of their own prophets and with the exact manner in which these prophecies had been traditionally interpreted. They were familiar with the Messianic hope, which the tribes of Israel had long cherished. The apostle Paul was outstandingly well furnished with a knowledge of the Old Testament Scriptures and his interpretation of these Scriptures deserves our attention, both from the standpoint of his natural qualifications and from the fact that he was inspired by the Holy Spirit.

This apostle, well taught in Rabbinical methods of interpretation and well qualified to express the hopes and the expectations of his people, appeared before Felix on a charge of heresy. His answer to this charge is most interesting: ". . . after the way which they call heresy, so worship I the God of my fathers, believing all things which are written in the law and in the prophets" (Acts 24:14). Here the issue is quite clear. It is not a case of denying what is written in the law and the prophets, but of different interpretation. A little later Paul appeared before King Agrippa in answer to a similar charge and his answer is equally significant. He tells the story of his conversion, his witnessing, and the consequent antagonism of his own people in the following words: "For these causes the Jews caught me in the temple, and went about to kill me. Having therefore obtained help of God, I continue unto this day, witnessing both to small and great, saying none other things than those which the prophets and Moses did say should come: That Christ should suffer, and that He should be the first that should rise from the dead, and should show light unto the people, and to the Gentiles" (Acts 26:21-23). Here again the great apostle affirms that he says "none other things than those which Moses and the prophets did say should come." The difference here was also a matter of interpretation. The carnally minded Jews interpreted the words of the prophets with absolute literalness and expected a literal kingdom. Paul gave the prophecies a spiritual interpretation and insisted that the kingdom of God was not quite in keeping with the expectations of the Jews. To him it was a spiritual kingdom. We believe that all the other apostles to whose writings we have access corroborate the words of Paul. It is, therefore, our duty, as it is our privilege, to search their writings in order to ascertain the nature of that kingdom which they expected to inherit.

The writer of the Epistle to the Hebrews is unknown by name. His identity is not important to our present purpose. We all agree that the Epistle was written to Hebrew Christians. It was written by someone who had a profound knowledge of the Hebrew Scriptures and Hebrew rituals. A Hebrew writing to Hebrews would be expected, as a matter of course, to refer to their mutual hopes and promises. It should be, therefore, instructive to see what the Epistle to the Hebrews has to say to those early Hebrew Christians.

The key word of this Epistle is the word *better*. It stresses the superiority of Christ to Moses. It shows how Jesus was made the mediator of a better covenant, and how much more potent His sacrifice is than of goats or of bullocks. His priesthood is shown to be superior to that of every other order; His gospel is revealed as being much better than the Mosaic law.

The Epistle sets forth gloriously the benefits of the Covenant of Grace and yet it cannot be but disappointing to all those who come to it looking for the promise of a Palestinian kingdom. Many of the people mentioned in the Epistle lived in the land of Canaan; but of them it is said, "But now they desire a better county, that is, an heavenly . . ." (Hebrews 11:16). The kingdom which God has prepared for His people is set forth here as being different from every other kingdom. Here we read God's promise to shake once more both heaven and earth, but at the same time we are told that the Hebrew Christians of that day had already received a kingdom which could not be moved. (See Hebrews 12:28.) It was said to them, "Ye are come to Mount Zion and unto the city of the living God, the heavenly Jerusalem, and to an innumerable company of angels" (Hebrews 12:22). These words are so plain that exposition is hardly necessary. They describe the children of God, the heirs of the Covenant of Grace, as having come to the real Mount Zion (and not "unto the mount that might be touched . . ." Hebrews 12:18); to the real Jerusalem, not the Palestinian Jerusalem; but the heavenly Jerusalem, the city of the living God. This clarifies one great truth. It teaches that just as Ishmael, the natural child, preceded Isaac, the child of promise; and that as Esau preceded Jacob, and in the course of time the elder served the younger; and the spiritual eclipsed the natural; so the natural mount Zion and Jerusalem and even the natural Israel have their spiritual counterparts. The mount Zion and the Jerusalem described in this passage are not identified by anyone as the locations of that name in Palestine. Mount Zion is the place where our king dwells, for the same passage describes believers as having come ". . . to Jesus the mediator of the new covenant," and, ". . . to the spirits of just men made perfect." (See Hebrews 12:23, 24.) They have come into that kingdom in which they belong to the great fellowship of the saints of all the ages. There is no promise of an earthly kingdom in the Epistle to the Hebrews, and that should constitute at least one good reason for not expecting to find it anywhere else.

We now turn to the Epistle of Paul to the Romans where much is said about the natural Israel. In the second and third

chapters of this Epistle, Paul teaches that both Jews and
Gentiles are by nature lost sinners and the whole world is guilty
before God. In the fourth and fifth chapters he speaks of
Abraham's justification by faith, and continues until the end
of chapter eight to stress the necessity and the benefits of
justification. In the ninth chapter, Paul laments the great
spiritual blindness of his kinsmen, according to the flesh, and
proceeds to show that the principle on which God deals with
both Jew and Gentile is the principle of sovereign grace. The
eleventh chapter of the Epistle to the Romans is a notable con-
tribution to our inquiry. In answer to his own question, "Hath
God cast away His people?" (Romans 11:1), Paul says, "Not
at all." Just as there were seven thousand faithful men of God
when Elijah could see none, "Even so then at this present time
also there is a remnant according to the election of grace. And
if by grace, then is it no more of works: otherwise grace is no
more grace . . ." (Romans 11:5-6). It is very important that
we should catch the thought in the apostle's mind at this point.
If we are asking whether God has cast off the natural Israel
when the nation rejected Christ, the answer is "there remains
a remnant" of the nation with whom God is dealing, no longer
on the basis of their racial origin, but "according to the election
of His grace." He has not cast off His people entirely, but He
no longer deals with them as a nation. He has a remnant of the
nation with whom He is dealing on the basis of grace and this
remnant constitutes the true Israel of God. Paul continues and
says the natural Israel ". . . hath not obtained that which he
seeketh for; but the election hath obtained it, and the rest were
blinded" (Romans 11:7). Here, then, is a truth that is plain
to him that understandeth. Israel looked for the fulfillment of
certain promises and did not obtain a fulfillment. The promises
are fulfilled spiritually to the elect.

Paul proceeds to draw a vivid and God-inspired picture of
God's relation to His people, under the figure of a good olive
tree, from which the natural branches had been broken off. The

natural branches are plainly the Jews, "the children of the kingdom." God, the husbandman, takes wild olive branches, the Gentiles, and grafts them into the stem where they partake of the root and fatness of the olive tree, the true vine which is Jesus Christ. (See Romans 11:17.) As the apostle watches the process he cries, "Behold therefore the goodness and the severity of God" (Romans 11:22). He dropped the native cultivated branches, which did not bring forth the expected fruit, and now He is grafting in the wild olive branches. However, the tree is not yet complete. There are some of those native branches lying about — dead to all appearances. Shall He not take some of them and graft them in. Yes, indeed, "And they also, if they abide not still in unbelief, shall be grafted in: for God is able to graft them in again" (Romans 11:23). The thought of this so stirs the apostle's heart that he says, "The restoration of them will be life from the dead." That is true of the restoration of every sinner. At present God is making up the tree. He is grafting in new branches, wild olive branches from the Gentiles, and native olive branches from the Jews. When the final act of grafting is completed, when the last member of the body of Christ is brought in and the elect of God accounted for, then "all Israel shall be saved," i. e., all those who have been grafted into the stem of the good olive tree. These will constitute the true Israel of God. The means of this ingathering is indicated in the same verse where the salvation of Israel is attributed to the fact that the Redeemer is coming out of Zion: "As it is written, There shall come out of Zion the Deliverer, and shall turn away ungodliness from Jacob" (Romans 11:26). This prophecy is found in Isaiah 59:20, but Paul does not quote it verbatim. Paul says that the Redeemer shall come out of Zion, rather than to Zion, as Isaiah says. The reason for this is that the Redeemer is already in Zion. This confirms the impression, which the New Testament so clearly gives in various passages, that Zion actually means the Christian church. Hence, the Hebrew Christians are told that they have already come to mount Zion, "not the mount that can be touched" (Hebrews 12:18). The implications of this fact are quite far reaching, for when Paul interprets Isaiah's prophecy to mean that Zion represents the church, that in itself should be a powerful determinant in our interpretation of prophecy.

We have seen that "all Israel," the elect of God, are to be saved. Dispensationalism contends that "all Israel" means the Hebrew nation. In the Scofield Reference Bible it says, "Israel is yet to be saved nationally."[1] That assumption has very great difficulties. Everyone would admit that millions of Jews have died in unbelief. If at the end they are all to be saved, there must be some provision for a second chance for all the unbelieving Jews of the past. This would also mean that for the present they are confined in some sort of a dispensational purgatory. There are those who say that the passage refers only to the Jews who shall be living at the time of Christ's return. This also has difficulties. It would mean that God, Who is no respecter of persons, would be a respecter of a certain generation. It is historically true that some generations have been blessed with spiritual revivals denied to their predecessors and successors, but there is neither precedent nor promise to support the idea that every soul of any race living at any given period of time shall be saved. Dispensationalists cite the latter part of Romans 11:25, "Blindness in part is happened unto Israel, until the fulness of the Gentiles be come in," with as much conviction as though it offered conclusive proof of the future conversion of the Jews. This passage does not even hint at any such probability. The idea of Jewish conversion is added by those who assume that it must be so. Furthermore, if "the fulness of the Gentiles" means the final ingathering from among the Gentiles, this would nullify the dispensational idea of the belated evangelization of the Gentiles by the "Jewish Remnant" in the tribulation of the end-time.

---

(1)   Scofield, C. I., THE SCOFIELD REFERENCE BIBLE, Page 1206

We do not discount the possibility that God may yet do a work of grace among the Jewish people; but in that event God will deal with them, as with their Gentile brethren, on the basis of sovereign grace involving individual election, calling, and justification. "For there is no difference between the Jew and the Greek; for the same Lord over all is rich unto all that call upon Him. For whosoever shall call upon the name of the Lord shall be saved" (Romans 10:12-13). It should be noted carefully that when in Romans eleven Paul speaks of the conversion of the Jews as a probability, he is speaking to the Gentiles in the hope that he might provoke the Jews to emulation: "If by any means I may provoke to emulation them which are my flesh, and might save some of them" (Romans 11:14). This is not, therefore, a definite promise of the conversion of the Jews so much as the expression of a great longing for it. It should also be noted that while the apostle regarded the conversion of the Jews as a possibility, he never hints at the possibility or probability of an earthly kingdom in Palestine for the Jews with Jesus as king. We suggest that anyone interested in this question, or having doubt about it, ascertain from Scripture what Paul means by "the hope of Israel." Nowhere is that hope defined as having its realization in an earthly kingdom, but in a resurrection of the dead.

A careful and unbiased examination of the remaining Epistles of Paul will confirm the impression that his view of the kingdom of God was of a strictly spiritual nature, and universal rather than national in scope. No one more than Paul stressed the fact that Christ, by the cross, abolished all partitions and dividing lines between Jews and Gentiles. If language has any meaning, Paul believed that the members of the true church of Jesus Christ constituted God's true Israel. He says, ". . . they are not all Israel, which are of Israel: neither, because they are the seed of Abraham, are they all children: but, in Isaac shall thy seed be called. That is, They which are the children of the flesh, these are not the children of God: but the children of the promise are counted for the seed" (Romans 9:6-8). "For he is not a Jew, which is one outwardly; . . . But he is a Jew, which is one inwardly: and circumcision is that of the heart, in the spirit, and not the letter" (Romans 2:28-29).

The views which Paul expresses in his other Epistles are in agreement with those which we have already reviewed in this chapter. His first Epistle to the Corinthians disposes of any fancied racial advantage, for he states, ". . . that flesh and blood cannot inherit the kingdom of God . . ." (I Corinthians 15:50).

The Epistle to the Galatians has great significance to those who would understand the relationship between God and the Jews during the Gospel age. Parts of this Epistle are frequently given a meaning foreign to its nature and content. We have heard Galatians 3:16 quoted with the emphasis of a conclusive statement in favor of the Jewish restoration. Here are the words: "Now to Abraham and his seed were the promises made. He saith not, And to seeds, as of many; but as of one, And to thy seed, which is Christ." Where anyone can find a promise of an earthly kingdom in this text or its context is a matter beyond our comprehension. In fact, the apostle closes the chapter with a most significant declaration: "There is neither Jew nor Greek, there is neither bond nor free, there is neither male nor female: for ye are all one in Christ Jesus. And if ye be Christ's, then are ye Abraham's seed, and heirs according to the promise" (Galatians 3:28-29).

The fourth chapter of Galatians is written to refute the contentions of Judaizers who were insisting on carrying into the new gospel dispensation the shadows and types which the gospel had abolished. Paul with irresistible logic tells them that those who are still under the law are represented by Ishmael, Abraham's child by the bond woman. Christians, whether Jew or Gentile, are represented by Isaac, the son of the free woman. So also Jerusalem, in Palestine, representing the natural Israel, is in bondage. The Jerusalem, which is from above, representing the spiritual Israel, the twice-born children of God, is free. Here again Paul clinches his argument by saying, "So then, brethren, we are not children of the bond woman, but of the free" (Galatians 4:31).

Paul writes to the Colossian believers and describes them as having been delivered from the power of darkness and translated into the kingdom of God's dear Son (See Colossians 1:13.) These believers were at that time in the kingdom. They were not, however, living in Palestine, but in Colosse. The New Testament can be searched with the greatest of care, but nowhere does one find in the Epistles, any more than in the Gospels, the slightest indication of a future restoration of a Jewish kingdom in Palestine. It is a matter of some importance to us that in the Epistles of Paul to the Thessalonians, and also in the Epistles of Peter, where so much is said of the Lord's return, a conspicuous silence is maintained on the matter of an earthly kingdom. It is never mentioned as a part of the blessed hope of the Church of God. Dr. T. T. Shields of Toronto expresses his convictions on this matter in strong language and also, we believe, with true spiritual discernment. He says, "Last Sunday evening I hope I made clear to you that the New Testament is silent as to the setting up of an earthly Jewish kingdom, the return of the Jews as a people to Palestine, the rebuilding of the temple, and the whole millennial program, as allegedly prophetically described — that the whole thing is utterly devoid of New Testament authority. It is not to be found explicitly or implicitly in the teachings of our Lord or His apostles. I venture to assert, indeed, that the teaching of the entire New Testament is to the contrary."[2] We find ourselves in hearty agreement with this great preacher and Bible student in these observations.

As we conclude this brief summary of New Testament teachings, we think that the words of the late Dr. W. M. Clow of

(2) Shields, T. T., THE GOSPEL WITNESS, Feb. 9, 1939, Page 3

Glasgow express the impressions which we have gained from our study: "This seems to me both evident and of the first importance, that the Atonement is the burden and message of the New Testament, its history, its reasoning, its experience; all center upon it. We usually find in any thing or in any man what we wish to see . . . I also may be mistaken, but if so, I am mistaken in the company of the great interpreters through all the centuries, when I say that the broad purpose of the New Testament is to tell us that Jesus died for our sins and rose again for our justification."[3]

(3) Clow. W. M., THE CROSS IN CHRISTIAN EXPERIENCE, Page 310-311

Chapter 7.

Millennial Theories

ANY discussion of millennial theories inevitably leads to a theological battleground on which one has to risk the sacrifice of reputation and popularity. This is a subject on which many Christians have no opinion, but on which others have formed such definite conclusions that they can hardly be induced to read or consider anything at variance with their present theories. This latter position is a rather precarious one. When anyone comes to the conclusion that his theory is absolutely right and every opinion to the contrary wrong, he is either assuming an unwarranted infallibility, or he must be absolutely certain that the Bible in its entirety supports his point of view. While few, if any, possess this assurance, it cannot be denied that many people are as dogmatic as though they did possess it. They are so sure of their eschatological point of view that they make it the yardstick of orthodoxy and the foundation upon which to build a real assurance of salvation.

We believe that an understanding of every phase of truth is important, but we just as steadfastly deny that any theory of the millennium is to be regarded as the proof of either orthodoxy or salvation. This applies to our own position, as well as to that of others. Dispensationalists do not readily share with us this admission, as may be proved from their writings. One such brother writes, "If the amillennialists are right, much precious sanctifying truth must needs be relinquished or explained away and . . . no one can speak with assurance as to his final salvation, because that matter awaits settlement at the judgment day, and the saints will not reign with Christ over this world because His kingdom will not be established until eternity begins."[1] Another writer presents a glowing word picture of the millennium and concludes with the words, "All of these promises must be fulfilled; if they are not we can have no confidence in the Bible. If this change in the earth, in its creatures, and in man himself does not take place then we might as well throw our Bibles away, for we can have no confidence at all in the promises concerning life after death, or in the keeping power of our risen Lord."[2] This is an exceedingly broad statement. We all believe that God's promises are to be fulfilled, but the author referred to insists they must be fulfilled according to his interpretation, if the Bible is not to be discarded, and the God of the Bible is to be considered worthy of our confidence. With reference to the statement that amillennialists cannot have assurance of final salvation, we can safely allow the Bible to speak for itself. We ask whether there is one single passage in the Bible where such an assurance is conditioned upon any theory of the millennium. We cannot imagine that the writers of these statements would attempt to give inquirers an assurance of salvation by a discourse on millennialism. The assurance of salvation is based upon the individual's acceptance of the finished work of Christ and the testimony of the Word of God to the believer's heart and conscience. Correct views of the millennium are important, as are correct views on any matter; but let us not insist that any one particular eschatological point of view is essential to salvation or to the assurance of salvation, for millions have gone out into eternity to be with Christ without any eschatological convictions, but satisfied with the assurance that Christ died in their room and stead.

As we come to the millennium, it is well to define our terms. The word *millennium* is a combination of two Latin words: *mille,* a thousand, and *annum,* a year — and literally means *a thousand years.* This period of a thousand years is said to

---

(1) Ironside, Harry A., THE LAMP OF PROPHECY, Page 117
(2) Barnhouse, D. G., HE CAME TO HIS OWN: BUT, Page 170

constitute the time of earth's golden age, and still in the future and supposed to precede the end of the world.

There are three major theological camps, each holding its own convictions on the millennium and each claiming to have found the answer to Pilate's question, "What is truth?" Perhaps the least vocal of these schools at the present time is that known as postmillennialism. The viewpoint represented by postmillenialsm is that the millennium will be past before the Lord returns to judge the earth. It is held that the church, by the preaching of the Gospel, shall regenerate and reform society and change the world to such an extent that war and want will be unknown, while peace, prosperity, and health will abound for one thousand years. At the end of that period Christ is expected to return, and His return will be coincidental with the resurrection of the dead, and the final judgment. The designation, *postmillennial,* applied to this school of Christian thought, is derived from its belief that the millennium will be past before Christ returns.

The postmillennial doctrine of the Lord's return was the popular doctrine several decades ago, and at that time it provided an incentive to missionary zeal and evangelistic fervor. The spread of the Gospel was regarded as hastening the millennium and the second coming of Christ. There was some justification for this optimism during the nineteenth century when the larger denominations were conservative and evangelistic, with the result that individual conversions were frequent and large scale religious revivals not uncommon. These circumstances might well inspire the hope that the preaching of the Gospel should usher in a golden age. It is not uncharitable to say that postmillennialism has changed, and that instead of presenting Christ's evangel today as a means of salvation and reformation, it has resorted to a humanistic gospel, the futility of which world events prove most emphatically. One learned representative of the postmillennial school asks, "Shall we still look to God to introduce a new order by catastrophic means, or shall we assume the responsibility of bringing about our own millennium?" He answers his own question in these words, "Evils still unconquered are to be eliminated by strenuous effort and gradual reform, rather than by the catastrophic intervention of Diety."[3] Others have gone further and look to the process of evolution to usher in the earth's golden age.

The above criticism does not apply to all who believe in postmillennialism. We have the warmest recollections of the church of our childhood in which this doctrine was proclaimed with great evangelistic fervor. A minister of that church defending postmillennialism, writes, "We must recognize, with the Bible in our hand, that the greatest divines of the past were not wrong in anticipating such a period of quiet for the church of God, ere her eternal rest in heaven."[4] One cannot but regret, however, that with the Bible in his hand, the writer did not produce chapter and verse to prove his contention. The obvious reason is that no such plain promise could be quoted from the New Testament, for neither Jesus Christ nor His apostles gave the slightest indication of any real rest for the church until she enters upon the rest prepared for the people of God on the other side of death. Our Lord's promise to His church in this world is tribulation, rather than ease and comfort. It was this conviction that led us to examine the other systems of eschatological thought in the light of Holy Scripture, and which led us to the conclusions which we express here. Whatever support postmillennialism may draw from its own interpretation of the Old Testament, we question seriously whether the New Testament gives any valid encouragement to this theory. We are not unmindful of the great galaxy of learned and Godly theologians who have been postmillennialists, but at the same time we must bow to a higher authority and confess our inability to find where the New Testament actually promises any golden age or happy millennium, prior to the

(3) Case, Shirley Jackson, THE MILLENNIAL HOPE, Page 229
(4) Campbell, Murdock, THY OWN SOUL ALSO, Page 66

return of the Lord Jesus Christ from heaven to welcome His people into the inheritance prepared for them from the foundation of the world.

Another millennial theory is premillennialism, so called because it insists that the Lord's return must precede the millennium. Premillennialists are not by any means unanimous on all details of premillennialism. It is, however, generally believed that the Lord Jesus Christ will come part way from heaven and in great secrecy will rapture His own church and simultaneously raise the dead in Christ to meet Him in the air, where they shall remain with Him for seven years, during which time there shall be unprecedented tribulation upon the earth. It is said that during this tribulation 144,000 Jews will be saved and they will carry on a vigorous work of evangelism, winning many souls out of an apostate world, despite the fact that the Holy Spirit and the church are taken out of the world prior to this. At the close of the seven years of tribulation Christ, with His church, will come down to earth and will rule the world from Jerusalem for one thousand years. During this thousand years Satan is to be bound and confined to the abyss, allowing the whole earth to enjoy peace and prosperity. For some reason, Satan is to be loosed at the close of the thousand years and will go out to deceive the nations. He is to incite a rebellion against Christ, but is to be destroyed. Then the wicked dead will be raised. The final judgment will take place and both righteous and wicked will be assigned to their eternal destinies. It would be but fair to state that this is a considerable expansion of historic premillennialism and one which some premillennialists do not accept in its totality.

It remains for us to mention the school known as amillennial, a term which indicates a denial of any future millennium of one thousand years' duration. The only new thing about this belief is its name. It is, in fact, the only eschatological point of view that one finds implied or taught in any of the great creeds of the church. The amillennialist believes definitely in the Lord's return, and in the resurrection of just and unjust at His coming, in the ushering in of the new heavens and the new earth in which righteousness shall dwell, when the fires of judgment have purged this world of every vestige of the curse of sin as the ancient world was purged by the flood. The amillennialist believes that the Lord Jesus will set up, not a kingdom of a thousand years' duration, but that His kingdom shall never be destroyed. He agrees with the ancient Seers and Psalmists that this kingdom shall be an everlasting kingdom, and that once and for all God shall wipe away the tears from His people's eyes. He believes that Paradise gained will henceforth by the grace and mercy of God be Paradise retained.

We have dismissed postmillennialism as being unscriptural and therefore unsatisfactory, at least so far as we are concerned. We now come to examine premillennialism. In doing so, we must take cognizance of certain circumstances which have greatly favored its acceptance and aided its popularity. There is a general idea abroad that premillennialism is the only alternative to postmillennialism, which seems to have no legitimate support in the New Testament, and which has so commonly degenerated into humanism. Premillennialism seems to offer a fairly plausible and acceptable interpretation of the prophetic Scriptures so long as one does not go into too much detail and refrains from asking too many awkward questions. This the average man will not do, for his interest in the Bible and in Christian theology will not impel him to make a careful study of the subject. These circumstances are further reinforced by the fact that the majority of the outstanding evangelists, who travel and preach all over the land, are premillennialists. Several of these evangelists are also editors of religious periodicals, which emphasize premillennialism as a phase of "the faith once delivered to the saints." The fact that these evangelists are known personally to a vast number of Christian people assures popularity and demand for their written sermons and expressed convictions. This situation is further strengthened by the fact that in the endeavor to escape the modernism of so many of the recognized theological seminaries, students for the ministry are trained in Bible Institutes which, with rare exceptions, hold the premillennial theory of the Lord's return. These facts and the Scofield Reference Bible with its "helps" would make it strange, indeed, if premillennialism did not make rapid progress.

The preceding chapters have dealt with some of the corollaries of premillennialism and, inasmuch as future chapters will deal with some more of its assumptions which cannot be treated within the scope of this chapter, we should like here to examine some of the implications of the supposed thousand-year reign of Jesus Christ in Jerusalem. It seems only reasonable that this assertion should raise a question regarding the nature and substance of our Lord's resurrected body, and the bodies of His saints who are expected to reign with Him in bodies fashioned like unto His glorious body. It is a fact that when our Lord rose from the grave the substance of His body was changed, so that normally He was invisible to human eyes. The disciples saw Him, felt Him, and were quite convinced of His identity. "He showed Himself alive after His passion by many infallible proofs." There was no doubt in their hearts but this was their Lord with His wounded hands and feet, and His lacerated side. He ate with them and appeared in their midst whenever it pleased Him to do so. He vanished out of their sight just as suddenly. In either case, there was no necessity for Him to enter or leave by the door. His resurrected body was of such a nature that material obstacles could not hinder its movements. It was not necessary to have the stone removed from the sepulchre in order that He should be able to come out, but that others might be able to go in. He could enter the room in which His disciples were gathered, with all the doors locked, and leave the room in the same manner.

It would also appear from the evidence that at times He was present with the disciples when they were not aware of His presence. When Thomas expressed his skepticism, Jesus seems to have heard him, for one week later Thomas was humbled as he heard His own expressions of unbelief quoted by the Master, who had not been present visibly. This surely suggests that in His resurrected body, our Lord was ordinarily invisible, but that He visibly manifested Himself to His disciples to strengthen their faith and to give the church in all ages a most adequate assurance of His resurrection. He actually ate in the presence of His disciples in His resurrected body, and this would seem to prove that His body was a material body. He challenged them to feel Him and be satisfied that He had flesh and bones. We are inclined to believe, however, that all this would hold true of the angels whose entertainment by Abraham is recorded in the eighteenth chapter of Genesis. So far as Abraham could see, they had natural bodies. They had to assume such bodies for the moment in order that Abraham might see them. Also in the nineteenth chapter of Genesis, we read of two angels who came to Lot in Sodom, "He made them a feast and did bake unleavened bread, and they did eat" (Genesis 19:3). This does not mean that the angels are always visible and tangible, or that they ordinarily eat. These celestial messengers made themselves visible to Abraham and to Lot for just that occasion. This, however, was the exception rather than the rule. Our risen Lord made Himself visible and tangible to His disciples as occasion required, but there is no record to show that others saw Him in the streets or anywhere else. His resurrected body was not dependent upon material sustenance, nor did He even need shelter or hospitality in any home after He rose from the dead.

These observations, based upon the plain teachings of Scripture, do not harmonize with the dispensational assumptions that Jesus Christ in His glorified body shall be housed in Jerusalem for one thousand years. There is no denying the fact that our Lord's return will be with unveiled glory and not in a state of humiliation as before. Dispensationalism does not solve the problem which this presents, nor does it seem to take into consideration the fact that there shall be a difference between the substance of the body which is mortal, and the body which shall be immortal. It is assumed that they shall be governed by the same conditions.

Another question closely related to the above emerges from the assertion that during the supposed millennium, resurrected and raptured saints will mingle freely and do business with those still in their mortal bodies. It is presumed that the resurrected saints shall rule the earth and enforce the laws of Christ during the millennium. Here again premillennialism makes no provision for the reconciliation of such irreconcilables as resurrected saints and mortal sinners in the same society. Modern spiritism thrives on its vain efforts and its pretenses at being able to establish communication between both classes now. It may be a cause for gratitude, rather than a cause for grief, that these efforts are not successful. If beings from the world of spirits came crowding in upon our world, that phenomenon might not be very convenient. It is a fact known everywhere that no small stir is sometimes caused in a neighborhood by the belief that a departed spirit is alleged to pay it an occasional visit. In some parts of the world, houses have stood vacant for years because people suspected the presence within them of a supernatural tenant. Premillennialism blends together the two classes without regard to the fact that one has gone through the process of death and resurrection, and the other has not, and that, therefore, their organisms are adapted to two different modes of existence — one material, and the other spiritual. In fact, premillennialism suggests a perfectly normal society made up of these differing elements during the millennium, and also anticipates that during this period the earth's population will greatly increase. This is bewildering when we remember that, according to premillennialism, the earth's millennial population will consist of vast numbers of resurrected saints, and that Jesus Christ plainly stated that there is no marrying or sex life in the resurrection. When the Sadducees asked Him which one of the seven husbands of a much widowed woman could claim her as his wife in the resurrection, He said, "Ye do err, not knowing the scriptures, nor the power of God. For in the resurrection they neither marry, nor are given in marriage, but are as the angels of God in heaven" (Matthew 22:29-30). If the resurrected saints are like the angels, how can it be imagined, much less asserted, that for one thousand years they shall mingle freely with men and women still in their carnal and mortal bodies, and live together under identical conditions? Premillennialism does not solve this question. The Bible does not solve it either, for the simple reason that the Bible does not propound it. It did not originate with the Bible.

All Christians believe that Jesus Christ is now at the right hand of God in heaven. The period of His humiliation ended with Calvary. Let us then imagine, if we can, what a transfer from the throne of His glory to an earthly throne in Palestine would mean to Him. His assumption of the most gloriously conceivable earthly position would be nothing short of another humiliation. Think of Christ having His throne in Jerusalem and the nations of the earth sending their accredited ministers to confer with Him, receiving His decrees with reluctance and offering Him lip service. This is the picture that dispensationalism paints, a picture of a thousand years of enforced righteousness during which Christ shall impose His sovereign will upon all and sundry, and after which they shall still rebel against Him. All of this seems so much at variance with the sense and meaning of the Scriptures that one wonders how it meets with acceptance among believers.

The Scriptures plainly reveal that when Christ returns, He will come "in all His glory" and not in any other way. What estimation, then, do men form of the brightness of His glory when they think He will still be as accessible as He was during the period of His humiliation? Will His glory be veiled when

He is enthroned among His resurrected people? We think not. If not, no man in his mortal body can endure His presence. His reign will, therefore, be among the immortals, and that is what the Bible teaches. When He comes in His glory, the very brightness of His coming will destroy the Antichrist and his forces: "And the kings of the earth, and the great men, and the rich men, and the chief captains, and the mighty men, and every bondman, and every free man, hid themselves in the dens and in the rocks of the mountains; And said to the mountains and the rocks, Fall on us, and hide us from the face of Him that sitteth on the throne, and from the wrath of the Lamb: For the great day of His wrath is come; and who shall be able to stand?" (Revelation 6:15-17). These words do not suggest that He will come making any offers or overtures to the world again. There will be no occasion or opportunity for nations or individuals to come to terms with Him then. There shall be no temporal reign of enforced righteousness, for He shall reign eternally over a people in whose hearts He has written His laws by the saving and sanctifying work of the Holy Spirit.

We bring this chapter to a close with the suggestion that the reader meditate upon the description of the Lord's return presented by the pen of inspiration in the second Epistle of Peter, chapter three, verses ten to thirteen. We do not say that this portion is any more Divinely inspired and authorized than Revelation twenty. We do say, however, that Peter's words contain no symbolism, and the book of Revelation certainly does. There is not even a premillennialist who will interpret the first six verses of Revelation twenty with absolute literalness. The language is highly symbolical. We ask, then, in the interest of truth, whether it be a proper practice for men of God to build doctrines upon symbols and twist other Scriptures into some sort of agreement, an agreement which we suspect to be rather unsatisfactory to themselves? The safe and the sane course is to interpret symbols in the light of plain and unambiguous statements of Scripture. This issue is of greater moment and importance than human pride or prejudice and we believe every man owes it to God, to himself, and to his fellow-men to refuse or abandon any position which is not adequately supported by plain and revealed truth.

Chapter 8.

The Seventy Weeks

IF ANY statement is frequently made and greatly emphasized, it stands a good chance of becoming accepted as truth
without too much question as to its origin and authority. This
is especially true when such a statement is issued from a pulpit
and over an open Bible. For such reasons, and in most cases
for no stronger reason, there is a general idea among Christians
that there is going to be a seven-year period of unparalleled
tribulation preceding the end of this age. This theory is supposedly derived from prophecies said to be contained in the
ninth chapter of Daniel, and also in the twenty-fourth chapter
of Matthew. This fact makes it easy for us to go directly to
the portions of the Word alleged to contain this doctrine. In
saying that people do not always have any stronger reason
than mere hearsay for what they believe, we are not being
unkind, for we have just read the following amazing words
from an outstanding minister and scholar who has written
many books on religion: "For twenty years, I also believed and
taught that the Roman Empire would be restored in the last
days of the age in which we live . . . I must confess that in so
doing I depended largely upon the ideas and interpretations
which I had imbibed from great and Godly teachers, in whom
I had unlimited confidence. I did not realize that I was teaching interpretations of the text in place of the Word itself, and
had never made an exhaustive study of the Scriptures involved
in this idea . . . I went over these prophecies again and was
finally led to see that my only authority for maintaining that
the Roman Empire would be rebuilt was a footnote in my
favorite edition of a study Bible. So for twenty years I had
taught as a prophecy of God's Word a human conclusion based

upon an ambiguous paragraph."[1] These challenging words reveal the proneness of even preachers of the Word of God to be satisfied with a baseless assumption which has no Scriptural foundation, except that it is approved and accepted by others. It is our conviction that this is true of much of the dispensational interpretation of the book of Daniel.

In this chapter we intend to deal briefly with only the closing verses of the ninth chapter, which dispensationalists describe as "the very backbone of prophecy." Those words would at least indicate the importance attached to their interpretation of the passages mentioned. Daniel was a captive in Babylon, and understood from the writings of the prophet Jeremiah that the period of the captivity was drawing near its end. This we know from Daniel's own words. (We suggest that this chapter should be read with your Bible open at Daniel nine, thus making the comments easier to follow.) Daniel realized that his people were soon to be released from their captivity and he began to review their history, to remember their sins, and to see how very faithfully God had fulfilled the words which He had spoken by Moses in bringing evil upon the people for their disobedience. The seventy years of bondage were now about to close and the people were to be released in accordance with the Word of the Lord. Daniel prayed that God might be pleased to bless them, that their Holy City might be rebuilt, and that once again they might be restored to Divine favor.

While thus praying and confessing his sins and the sins of his people, Daniel had a vision in which the angel Gabriel came to him and to quote Daniel's own words: "And he informed me, and talked with me, and said, O Daniel, I am now come forth to give thee skill and understanding . . . Seventy weeks are determined upon thy people and upon thy holy city, to finish the transgression, and to make an end of sins, and to make reconciliation for iniquity, and to bring in ever-

(1)   Rimmer, Harry, THE COMING LEAGUE AND ROMAN DREAM, Page 42 and 44

lasting righteousness, and to seal up the vision and prophecy, and to anoint the most Holy" (Daniel 9:22, 24). This statement of what should happen during the seventy weeks was followed by an announcement of when the seventy weeks should begin, and it is to be reasonably assumed that when one knows when one week or seventy weeks will begin, one knows when they will end. The seventy weeks were weeks of years, an interpretation which is not without Biblical sanction and precedent. In Genesis 29:27, we find Jacob and Laban negotiating for Rachel. Laban says, "Fulfill her week, and we will give thee this also for the service which thou shalt serve with me yet seven other years." This, at least, is one precedent for the application of the word *week* to the period of seven years. Furthermore, the word translated week is *shabua* and simply means *a seven* or *heptad,* not necessarily of days. This interpretation of seventy heptads of years does no injury to this truth, and is generally accepted by all schools.

We are now to study these verses in Daniel nine and, as we review them in the greater light of the New Testament, see whether or not they would seem to suggest anything like the intricate eschatological system based upon them. Six things are here predicted to take place during the seventy weeks. We have actually submitted some of these to young Christians, who readily associated them with the atoning work of the Lord Jesus Christ. The seventy weeks were determined upon Daniel's people "to finish the transgression." The reader can look up the words *transgress* and *transgression* in the Bible and will find that the transgression of Israel as a nation was the constant burden and heartbreak of the prophets of Israel. In the eleventh verse of this chapter, Daniel says, "Yea, all Israel have transgressed Thy law, even by departing, that they might not obey Thy voice: therefore the curse is poured upon us, and the oath that is written in the law of Moses the servant of God, because we have sinned against Him." It was their transgressions that made the Israelites captives in Babylon.

Daniel knew this too well. In this instance, however, the angel
Gabriel reveals to Daniel that Israel's crowning transgression
would be the rejection and death of Israel's Messiah. That was
the nation's last outstanding act as a nation. The people,
through their leaders, declared that they had no king but
Caesar, and they have been trodden under the heels of a suc-
cession of Caesars ever since. This act wrote the word *finis* to
a long list of successive national apostasies; and one can surely
see in this case what Gabriel meant by saying, "Seventy weeks
are determined upon thy people and upon thy holy city, to
finish the transgression." This marked the end of national
transgression and the final rejection of God by the nation.

As we come to examine the remaining part of this verse, we
feel like exclaiming with Paul, "O the depth of the riches both
of the wisdom and knowledge of God! how unsearchable are His
judgments, and His ways past finding out! For who hath known
the mind of the Lord? or who hath been His counsellor?"
(Romans 11:33-34). Israel's diabolical act in taking their
Messiah with wicked hands and having Him crucified and slain
was the very act that opened the way of salvation to mankind.
This final national transgression, having its climax at the place
called Calvary, was the act Divinely designed "to make an end
of sins and to make reconciliation for iniquity, and to bring
in everlasting righteousness." How sickening it must be to
many of the Lord's people, how subversive of truth and how
insulting to the Lord Himself to insist that this has not yet
happened, but is still in the future! It is difficult, indeed, to
understand how any instructed child of God can miss the
meaning of these words when Scripture and Christian faith
comfort the believing soul day by day with the assurance that
once and for all Christ has made an end of sins, made reconciliation for iniquity, and brought in everlasting righteousness. In
addition to the foregoing, the period of the seventy weeks was
to include the sealing up of prophecy which was fulfilled by the
closing of the Old Testament prophetic system. "The anointing

of the most Holy" was simply the anointing of Him who declared publicly, "The spirit of the Lord is upon me, because He hath ANOINTED me to preach the gospel to the poor . . ." (Luke 4:18).

The angel Gabriel, having given Daniel a general statement of the events that should come to pass during the seventy weeks, then proceeded to tell him when the seventy weeks were to begin and how they were to be divided and punctuated by events of unsurpassed importance. The seventy weeks were to begin with the decree of Cyrus to liberate the Jews from their captivity in Babylon and to rebuild Jerusalem. How marvelous that before Cyrus was born, God named him to Isaiah as "the man who will perform my pleasure." (See Isaiah 44:28 and 45:1-5.) It must have thrilled Daniel's heart to see Cyrus coming to power, because Daniel knew that the Word of God should be fulfilled. The first chapter in the book of Ezra gives us the interesting information that Cyrus issued the liberating decree, thus giving the Jews their freedom and fulfilling the Word of God spoken by Jeremiah, the Prophet. Students of prophecy are not by any means unanimous in the opinion that this was the decree referred to by Daniel, and to identify the decree is not at all important to us. The important matter is "that from the going forth of the commandment to restore and build Jerusalem unto the Messiah the Prince shall be seven weeks, and threescore and two weeks" (Daniel 9:25).

The seventy weeks were to be divided into three periods. The first period consisted of seven weeks, or forty-nine years, during which the city of Jerusalem was to be rebuilt. From the time that the city should be rebuilt until the coming of the Messiah should be sixty-two weeks. The seven weeks of years required for the rebuilding of the city and sixty-two weeks of years extending from that time until the day of Christ account for sixty-nine prophetic weeks, "and after threescore and two weeks" (in addition to the first seven) "shall Messiah be cut off, but not for Himself" (Daniel 9:26). It is scarcely necessary to comment on the meaning of this passage. We all know that the Messiah was cut off. The question that is difficult to answer is why, when Messiah was cut off after the sixty-ninth week, dispensationalists deny that it happened in the seventieth week. The teaching of dispensationalism is that while sixty-nine of the seventy weeks were fulfilled in proper and natural chronological order, the seventieth week was separated from the other sixty-nine by twenty centuries. The logic employed here is, we believe, without precedent. It has neither precedent nor pattern in the Word of God, and is hardly in keeping with the vaunted literalism of our dispensational brethren. Let us suppose for a moment that this manner of interpretation were applied to other parts of Scripture. God told Abraham that his seed should be in bondage in Egypt for four hundred years, but there is no record of any believer manipulating those figures to include an extra twenty centuries for good measure. God told Jeremiah that the captivity in Babylon would last seventy years, and Daniel understood by the writings of Jeremiah that the captivity was about to end. Suppose Daniel had in dispensational fashion believed that an unreckoned period of time should separate the seventieth year from the sixty-ninth year of the captivity in Babylon — say a period of twenty centuries — then surely prophecy would become an absurdity. It is contended that the angel separated the seventieth week of Daniel's prophecy from the rest for no other purpose than that there should be "a great parenthesis" between them. We answer, however, that the angel separated the first seven weeks from th following sixty-two weeks, but there was no intervening period or parenthesis between them. The first seven weeks of years were notable because of the events which transpired during those weeks. Likewise, the seventieth week was separated from the other sixty-nine because that seventieth week was the most eventful in all of human history and was, in fact, the week that so divided human history that henceforth events became dated *A. D., Anno Domini, the year of our Lord* instead of *B. C., Before Christ.* Men are surely taking strange liberties with the truth of God when they laboriously build a mountain of doctrine upon a molehill of symbolism or conjecture.

There is no authority in Scripture for the assumption that the seventieth week of Daniel is still in the future. On the contrary, there is satisfactory and abundant proof that the seventieth week followed the sixty-ninth without any break, as every rule of logic and history would demand. Surely if any man, to say nothing of an angel acting as the spokesman of the Most High, were to guarantee and to determine something to happen within seventy weeks, it could not reasonably be interpreted as meaning seventy weeks plus twenty centuries. It is universally agreed that the events predicted for the seven-week period and the sixty-two weeks period following it have taken place; yet in some quarters it is denied, regardless of evidence to the contrary, that the events of the seventieth week have followed those of the sixty-ninth. We listened just recently to a radio address on the seventieth week of Daniel and availed ourselves of the invitation to write for a free copy in order to be sure that we heard correctly. We give here a quotation of the incredible teaching that came to us over one of the national networks: "Four hundred and eighty-three of the four hundred and ninety years determined upon the nation of Israel and Jerusalem have been fulfilled and terminated at the crucifixion of the Lord Jesus Christ. Then God began to deal with the church, and Israel as a nation was set aside and the kingdom postponed until God's purpose for the church has been fully accomplished, and she shall be taken out and God will begin dealing with Israel for the last and glorious week of the seventy weeks of Daniel. Now, will you notice that the seventy weeks are divided into three parts, the first section lasting for seven weeks, or forty-nine years, the second part lasting for sixty-two weeks, or four hundred thirty-four years, leaving the last one of these weeks, the seventieth week of seven years still unfulfilled, even up until this present time."[2] The sad part of all this is that men attach to such baseless interpretations the certainty and infallibility which belongs only to the Word of God itself and that men are as positive and as dogmatic in the proclamation of human concoctions and fanciful interpretations as they could possibly be in the propagation of established truth. Far be it from us to suspect insincerity on the part of any fellow believer, but we have seriously wondered whether or not some men willfully and stubbornly refuse to accept truth and cling to falsehood, rather than admit that they have been misinformed.

Speculation reaches a climax and history is utterly disregarded in the interpretation of the latter part of Daniel 9:26: ". . . the people of the prince that shall come shall destroy the city and the sanctuary; and the end thereof shall be with a flood, and unto the end of the war desolations are determined." There are few events recorded in all the annals of human history more dreadful than the literal fulfillment of these words, as seen in the utter destruction of Jerusalem under the Roman general Titus in the year seventy A. D. Dispensational conjecture is at its best in interpreting this verse. It admits the undeniable, that the Romans did destroy Jerusalem in the year seventy A. D. by the people of "the prince which is to come," but insists that the prince himself is still in the future. In support of this we quote the words of a leading exponent of this theory: "Once more the head of the restored Roman Empire, as it is to be during the time of the end, looms up before us in the last two verses of this chapter. The people of the coming prince, the Romans, were to come and destroy both city and temple after Messiah had been cut off and had nothing for himself . . . The Romans under Titus Vespasianus in the year seventy fulfilled this prediction and in that year the prophecy before us became history. But Titus is not 'the prince that shall come.' "[3]

---

(2) DeHaan, M. R., THE SEVENTY WEEKS OF DANIEL, Page 34
(3) Gaebelein, A. C., REVELATION, Page 190

Dispensationalism is so determined to ignore the fact that this prophecy was fulfilled in seventy A. D. that it must not only find a future prince to fulfill it, but it must provide also an empire for that prince, and thus must teach the revival and reconstruction of the ancient Roman Empire, for which there is no support in Scripture except, as had been pointed out at the beginning of this chapter, a footnote in a certain edition of the Bible. Two decades ago men were so confident of this that the invasion of Ethiopia by the ill-fated Benito Mussolini was hailed as the beginning of the end. We have heard such statements made from the pulpit by men who were privileged to address thousands of Bible-believing people who were inclined to accept without question conjectures which were given the sanction and authority of Biblical interpretation. Subsequent events must have convinced such men of the folly of "being wise above that which is written," and have caused the withdrawal from circulation of some highly speculative books on prophecy.

The closing verse of Daniel nine has long been a stronghold for dispensationalism. Here, it is alleged, the angel describes and predicts the coming of Antichrist. Instead of reading out of the passage what it contains, the tendency is to read into it what some people think it ought to teach. Dispensationalism maintains that Daniel 9:27 teaches that a great prince shall rise in the last days with whom apostate Jews will make a covenant under which they will be permitted to continue their sacrificial rites. "In the midst of the week he shall cause the sacrifice and the oblation to cease," and shall compel men to worship himself.

As we submit what we believe to be the Scriptural meaning of the passage, we have pleasure in referring to *Cowles Commentary* and also to the book *Daniel the Beloved,* by Dr. W. M. Taylor, both of which we have consulted. Dr. Taylor quotes Dr. Cowles on this verse, as follows: "One seven shall make the covenant effective to many. The middle of the seven shall make sacrifice and offerings cease: then down upon the summit of the abomination comes the desolator, even till a complete destruction, determined, shall be poured upon the desolate."[4] It is clear, then, that Jesus Christ began His ministry at the end of the sixty-ninth and at the beginning of the seventieth week of Daniel's prophecy. During the first half of the seventieth week He confirmed the covenant to as many as received Him. While instituting the Last Supper at the close of that period, He spoke these unforgettable words, "For this is my blood of the New Covenant which is shed for the remission of sins" (Matthew 26:28). This covenant is not broken and never shall be, for it is ratified and sealed by His blood. In like manner, He caused the sacrifice and oblation to cease by offering Himself as a sacrifice which fulfilled every shadow, sign, and symbol of the Old Testament ritual. It was a remarkable fact that those associated with Him, while reared in a system which demanded repeated sacrifices, never offered another sacrifice after He had been offered up as the Lamb of God. It seems clear to us that the seventieth week of Daniel's prophecy is very distinctly marked here by this unmistakable event which took place in the midst of the week and which so marvelously fulfilled Gabriel's prediction. In the midst of the week our Lord, by His death, abolished the necessity of further sacrifice. During the remainder of the seventieth week the Gospel continued to be preached to the Jews whose hearts were being constantly hardened in consequence of their rejection of the Messiah, and whose desolation was now hastening on as determined.

As we follow these great events of the Gospel age in this prophecy, we cannot but be impressed and solemnized as we see God's faithfulness to His Word. The events of the seventieth week are not in the future. They followed the events of the sixty-ninth week in natural and logical sequence. It is not without sorrow of heart, therefore, that we listen to men, whose sincerity we do not question, emphasizing the fact that an end is not made to sin, that everlasting righteousness is yet to be brought in, and going so far as to attribute to a wicked Antichrist that which our glorious Lord has brought about by His sacrifice on the cross, the abolition of the oblation and sacrifice.

Chapter 9.

The Great Tribulation

WE HAVE observed that the ninth chapter of Daniel gave definite predictions of the Messiah, and of certain events associated with the termination of His earthly ministry. Those who insist that the seventy weeks of Daniel's prophecy have to do with the Hebrew people are quite justified in so doing. The ninth chapter of Daniel is, in fact, a prophecy of the nation's reaction to the promised Messiah and of Jewry's crowning transgression, the rejection of the Son of God, with its tragic aftermath. The Lord Jesus wept bitter tears as He looked down upon the city of Jerusalem from the Mount of Olives and said, "O Jerusalem, Jerusalem, thou that killest the prophets, and stonest them which are sent unto thee, how often would I have gathered thy children together, even as a hen gathereth her chickens under her wings, and ye would not! Behold, your house is left unto you desolate" (Matthew 23: 37, 38).

This desolation, which should come upon Jerusalem through her rejection of Christ, had been plainly foretold by Daniel and later confirmed by our Lord Himself, when He stated that this devastation should be associated with tribulation of such a nature as had never been experienced until then, and such as should never be paralleled in all the remaining years of time. We believe that it was the nature, rather than the magnitude, of the tribulation that our Lord had in mind, and which He said was to be without equal in all of history.

A great number of Christian people have associated what they call "The Great Tribulation" with the close of the Gospel dispensation. This theory is rather widely accepted and for the most part without question and without examination. We confess that we, too, acquiesced in this opinion before we made a thorough study of it. We accepted it because of our confidence in those who taught it, and because it seemed to be so universally accepted by Christians. We are now convinced, however, that a careful examination of Matthew twenty-four and of other similar passages bearing upon the destruction of Jerusalem will reveal that the tribulation of which they speak is not necessarily characteristic of the end of the world, but has been a very definite feature of the end of the Hebrew nation as such.

All readers of the New Testament know that Jesus Christ promised His disciples that in this world they should have tribulation. (See John 16:33.) On the very threshold of discipleship Jesus placed a cross, insisting that cross-bearing was involved in allegiance to Him. This cross-bearing symbolizes suffering, and the individual Christian's cross is the sum total of what he suffers because of his loyalty to Christ. Genuine godliness can expect suffering in this world. These sufferings are not the unprecedented tribulation described in Mathew twenty-four, nor are they at all related to the abominations and desolation predicted in the book of Daniel. These Scriptures give vivid descriptions and predictions of a specific judgment about to come upon a nation because of its iniquity.

The difficulties encountered in seeking to interpret Matthew twenty-four make it very necessary for one to have Divine light and guidance as he carefully compares Scripture with Scripture. Here one must endeavor to determine how certain words have been used in other portions of Scripture, and allow these words to have the same meaning here as elsewhere. We hope to abide by this rule in the interpretation which follows.

Our Lord's Olivet discourse contained in the twenty-fourth chapter of Matthew immediately followed His denunciation of the Scribes and Pharisees contained in the previous chapter. There He urges them to fill up the measure of their fathers. (See Matthew 23:32.) The idea is that the cup of iniquity of the Jewish nation is about to be filled and that upon the generation then living "may come all the righteous blood shed upon the earth, from the blood of righteous Abel unto the blood of Zacharias son of Barachias, whom ye slew between the temple and the altar. Verily I say unto you, All these things shall come upon this generation" (Matthew 23:36, 36).

This latter prediction is repeated in Matthew 24:34 where Jesus says, "Verily I say unto you, This generation shall not pass, till all these things be fulfilled." The meaning of this sentence seems quite obvious, but it is difficult to see how "all these things" were really fulfilled during the lifetime of that generation. Some interpreters have tried to overcome this obstacle by substituting the idea of race, nation, stock or family, for generation. They insist that what Jesus really meant was that the Jews, as a race, should not pass away until these things should be fulfilled. The Scofield Reference Bible states that the Greek word *genea* translated *generation* means "race, kind, family, stock or breed."[1] To this Dr. Scofield adds parenthetically "so all lexicons." It may be that some lexicons support this opinion, but certainly not "all lexicons." We have before us Thayer's Greek-English Lexicon of the New Testament, a very able and reliable work in this field. On page 112 of this volume it is distinctly stated that the word *genea* translated *generation* in Matthew 23:36 and in Matthew 23:34 means "the Jewish race at one and the same period" or "the whole multitude of men at the same time." This interpretation seems both obvious and reasonable.

It may be profitable and convincing to the reader to see how the word *generation* is used in other parts of Matthew's Gospel. In Matthew 1:17 we read, "so all the generations from Abraham to David are fourteen generations; and from David until the carrying away into Babylon are fourteen generations; and from the carrying away into Babylon unto Christ are fourteen generations." Here one finds the same Greek word used, but no one would suggest that it be translated "fourteen races, kinds, families, stocks or breeds." In Matthew 11:16 Jesus

---

(1) Scofield, C. I., THE SCOFIELD REFERENCE BIBLE, Page 1034

asked, "But whereunto shall I liken this generation?" It is plain to anyone that He is speaking of the people then living and describing their attitude toward John the Baptist and Himself. Again in Matthew 12:39-43 Jesus speaks of an adulterous generation and says that the men of Nineveh and the queen of the south shall rise against it. The men of Nineveh repented at the preaching of Jonah, and a greater than Jonah preached to that generation. The queen of the South came from the uttermost parts of the earth to hear the wisdom of Solomon, and a greater than Solomon was available to that generation. In each case Jesus Christ is using the word *generation* to describe His contemporaries, and we question seriously if in any of the four Gospels the word is used with any other meaning. This, then, should convince us beyond a doubt that our Lord is not speaking of a race, but that He is speaking of the people living at that time when He says, "Verily I say unto you, This generation shall not pass, till all these things be fulfilled" (Matthew 24:34).

All this brings us face to face with the fact that Jesus Christ promised certain things and expected these promises to be fulfilled during that generation. If we accept this as the meaning of Matthew 24:34, we must at once try to determine what is meant by "these things" of which Christ spoke. The Scofield Reference Bible says, "none of these things i.e. the world-wide preaching of the kingdom, the Great Tribulation, the return of the Lord in visible glory, and the regathering of the elect occurred at the destruction of Jerusalem by Titus in A.D. 70. The promise is therefore that the generation, nation or family of Israel will be preserved unto 'these things.' "[2]

In this study we take the position that Matthew 24:34, in which our Lord speaks of the generation then living, is the time text of the chapter and that our Lord's predictions up to that point have to do with the destruction of Jerusalem, which took place in the year 70 A. D. All His predictions concerning that notable event are clear and definite.

(2) Scofield, C. I., THE SCOFIELD REFERENCE BIBLE, Page 1034

Having stated our conviction we go back to Matthew 23:38 where our Lord, after His bitter denunciation of the Scribes and Pharisees, pronounced upon them the sentence of doom, saying, "Behold, your house is left unto you desolate." Having spoken these words, "Jesus went out, and departed from the temple" (Matthew 24:1). His pronouncement brought great perplexity to the minds of His disciples who were inclined to believe that the temple was as permanent as the world itself, and therefore felt that the destruction of the temple would mark the end of the world. In an endeavor to draw from Him some further explanation of this prediction of desolation the disciples directed His attention to the buildings of the temple, only to hear the terrible announcement that there should not be left one stone upon another. This brought from them the question, "Tell us, when shall these things be? and what shall be the sign of thy coming, and of the end of the world?" (Matthew 24:3). It is quite evident from the records of Mark and Luke that the emphasis of this question was on the destruction of Jerusalem. Neither one of these writers reports that part of the question which had reference to the end of the world. The disciples in their thinking had connected together the destruction of Jerusalem and the end of the world. They were not intentionally asking questions about a series of separated and unrelated events, but about that of which they had conceived as one and the same event — the destruction of Jerusalem and the end of the world. Mark and Luke do not seem to regard this as a two-fold question. Mark tells us that "Peter and James and John and Andrew asked Him privately, Tell us, when shall these things be? and, what shall be the sign when all these things shall be fulfilled?" Mark 13:34). Luke reports the question in almost identical terms, omitting any reference to the end of the world.

The Lord Jesus gave immediate answer to the question asked by His four disciples and one can see in His detailed answer His concern and anxiety lest His disciples should be deceived into thinking that the end of the world and His return should be coincidental with the destruction of Jerusalem. That calamity was to be presaged by signs which should be altogether unmistakable. Our Lord enumerated them in detail as they led up to the terrible desolation about to befall His nation and declared emphatically that these things should be fulfilled within a generation, or within the life tenure of the people living at that time. He has never manifested such definiteness when discussing the end of the world. In this case the security and the preparedness of His disciples required that they should know when the city was to fall, in order that the godly remnant might escape, which purpose was accomplished when the time came.

We now come to discuss "these things" which He mentioned as the signs of Jerusalem's approaching desolation. We have first His prophecy of false christs: "For many shall come in my name, saying, I am Christ; and shall deceive many" (Matthew 24:5). History has preserved for us the names of some of those deceivers, who drew multitudes after them by their claims to heavenly origin and spiritual power, while naturally there were many whose names no historian has recorded. In the book of Acts we read, "But there was a certain man, called Simon, which beforetime in the same city used sorcery, and bewitched the people of Samaria, giving out that himself was some great one; To whom they all gave heed, from the least to the greatest, saying, This man is the great power of God" (Acts 8:9, 10). Iranaeus says, "Simon claimed to be the Son of God and the creator of the angels." Those who are familiar with the works of Josephus, the Jewish historian, will find descriptions of many other deceivers of that time. The following quotations may sufficiently prove this point: "There was also another body of wicked men gotten together not so impure in their actions, but more wicked in their intentions . . . these were such men as deceived and deluded the people under pretense of Divine inspiration . . .

These prevailed with the multitude to act like mad men and went before them into the wilderness . . . There was also an Egyptian false prophet that did the Jews more mischief than the former because he was a cheat and got together thirty thousand men that were deluded by him. These he led round about from the wilderness to the mount, which was called the Mount of Olives."[3] Many other quotations could be given to show that false messiahs became quite numerous during these intervening years between the crucifixion of Christ and the destruction of Jerusalem. The references already cited give some idea of the reason for our Lord's warning, "Wherefore if they shall say unto you, Behold, he is in the desert; go not forth" (Matthew 24:26). His disciples were definitely warned by Him that the rise of such deceivers would be a characteristic of that age.

The promise of false christs was followed by promises of wars, pestilences, earthquakes, famines, and persecutions. When Christ delivered His Olivet discourse, the Roman Empire was at peace, but very shortly afterwards the vast Roman army was challenged by revolts and insurrections in all parts of the empire. Scores of thousands of Jews were slain in Syria and Selucia, while in Rome itself four emperors met death by violence in the short period of eighteen months. Wars, and rumors of wars, convulsed the Roman world. Earthquakes became numerous. It is a matter of historical record that during this period there had been earthquakes in Crete, Smyrna, Miletus, Samos, Laodicea, Rome and Judea. In addition to these disturbances both famine and persecution were rampant, as may be seen by reading the book of Acts.

Our Lord follows these predictions with a definite promise that "the gospel of the kingdom shall be preached in all the world for a witness" (Matthew 24:14). Many people have the impression that this applies to the modern world, and that Christ cannot come again until the gospel has been

(3) Josephus, WARS OF THE JEWS, Book II

preached to all the world. Let us inquire what He meant and what His disciples understood by these words of His. It can be proved beyond contradiction that to the disciples of Jesus Christ the world was simply the Roman Empire. For example, Luke tells us that "There went out a decree from Caesar Augustus that all the world should be taxed . . . And all went to be taxed, everyone to his own city" (Luke 2:1 and 3). The same writer tells us in another place of the day of Pentecost and says, "There were dwelling at Jerusalem Jews, devout men, out of every nation under heaven" (Acts 2:5). The apostle Paul wrote a letter to the church in Rome in which he says, "Your faith is spoken of throughout the whole world" (Romans 1:8). In his letter to the Colossians he speaks of the gospel "Which is come unto you, as it is in all the world" (Colossians 1:6), while in the twenty-third verse of the same chapter he speaks of "the gospel which ye have heard, and which was preached to every creature which is under heaven." Scoffers and infidels have pointed to these passages as some of the so-called mistakes of the Bible, contending that not a fraction of the whole world could have been taxed by Caesar Augustus, and that the gospel had touched but a small portion of the world in Paul's day. This is due to their failure to understand that Paul's world was just the vast Roman Empire, for Rome had conquered every part of the then known world. There is every reason to believe that all parts of the Roman world had heard the gospel prior to the destruction of Jerusalem, and that this was what our Lord had predicted to His disciples.

The next sign mentioned by our Lord as a warning of imminent danger was "the abomination of desolation spoken of by Daniel the Prophet." This abomination of desolation was to stand in the holy place. Dispensationalism interprets this sign as a future desecration of the temple by the Antichrist. In this connection it is instructive to turn to the records of Mark and Luke. Mark says, "But when ye shall see the abomination of desolation, spoken of by Daniel the Prophet, standing where it ought not, (let him that readeth understand)" (Mark 13:14). Luke's rendering is still different: "And when ye shall see Jerusalem compassed with armies, then know that the desolation thereof is nigh" (Luke 21:20). It seems clear that Luke interpreted the "abomination of desolation" to mean the Roman army, and was directed by the spirit of God to give the interpretation of our Lord's words instead of the words themselves. Dr. G. Campbell Morgan agrees that the abomination of desolation definitely means the Roman armies, but suggests that the holy place mentioned in Matthew's Gospel is the temple. (See G. Campbell Morgan, *Parables and Metaphors of Our Lord*, Page 143.) This leaves room for the objection that inasmuch, as the abomination of desolation was a sign warning believers to escape, their escape would not be possible once the temple, the last Jewish stronghold, was invaded by the Roman legions. The explanation is that while it is the army which is described as the "abomination of desolation," the "holy place" mentioned is not the temple. There was a specific word for the Holy of Holies, and it is not used in any of the three records of our Lord's conversation. What is actually meant is that the army will be seen in the holy locality, vicinity, or environment, "where it ought not to be." Any part of Jerusalem, or its environs, would have been holy to the Jews, and the reference here is to the outlying topography of Jerusalem itself. Neither Mark nor Luke seem to find any difficulty in the interpretation of this passage. They correctly take for granted that the Roman army is the "abomination of desolation." History reveals why the Roman army was called the abomination of desolation. It is a well known fact that the Roman soldiers carried ensigns consisting of eagles and images of the emperor to which divine honors were paid by the army. No greater abomination could possibly meet the eye of a Jew than ensigns to which idolatrous worship was offered. This was what happened at the fall of Jerusalem as told by the eye-witness Flavius Josephus: "And now the Romans, upon the flight of the seditious from the city, and upon the burning of the holy house itself, and of all the buildings round about it, brought their ensigns to the temple, and set them over against its eastern gate; and there did they offer sacrifices to them." This was the climax of the abomination of desolation, and such desolation as never was experienced by any other city in the history of the world. At the first sign of it, no time was to be lost. Men working in the fields were not to return home for their personal effects, and those reclining on the flat roofs of their houses were to run along the housetops to expedite their escape from the doomed city. The inhabitants of Jerusalem were at once to take to the Mountains of Judea. It is very significant that the disciples who believed the words of Christ, and looked for those signs, were able to make good their escape. Our gracious Lord, foreseeing this terrible catastrophe, added these sorrowful words, "Woe unto them that are with child, and to them that give suck in those days." This does not have any application to the end of the world, but it did greatly intensify mental and physical suffering during the siege of Jerusalem.

Unprecedented tribulation was a further prediction for those days. We are living in times when men and women have suffered some of the worst tortures imaginable. It would be difficult for human ingenuity to devise anything more diabolical than the atrocities practiced in European prison camps in recent years. With that in mind, some of our brethren deny that the destruction of Jerusalem involved any tribulation which has not been matched in more recent times, and maintain that the "great tribulation" is still in the future. The nature of Jerusalem's tribulation was more terrible than any the world has ever known. There never has been another siege in which men and women were afflicted and tormented more by their friends than by their enemies. Historians estimated that three million people were gathered in Jerusalem for the Jewish Passover when the rioting began. The inhabitants of the city divided themselves into fighting factions, falling upon each other, and showing neither mercy for the living nor respect for the dead.

Here it might be of interest to quote the words of Josephus, who is probably our best authority on the history of that particular period. Josephus, a Jew, was born in the year 37 A.D. and died about the year 100 A.D. He was at one time governor of Galilee, and was taken prisoner by the Romans prior to the siege of Jerusalem. His captors, impressed by his ability, made him mediator between themselves and the Jews. His writings cannot be suspected of any bias in favor of Christianity for he was not himself a Christian. We commend his writings to anyone interested in the history of this period, as only fragmentary quotations can be given here. His impressions of Jerusalem's tribulation may be judged from the words which follow: "It is impossible to go distinctly over every instance of these men's iniquity. I shall, therefore, speak my mind here at once briefly: — That neither did any other city ever suffer such miseries, nor did any age ever breed a generation more fruitful in wickedness than this was, from the beginning of the world." Let it be remembered that here Josephus is speaking of the Jews and not of the Romans. These Jews he describes under the title of "the seditious" and, speaking of them further, states: "The madness of the seditious did also increase together with their famine, and both those miseries were every day inflamed more and more . . . Many there were indeed, who sold what they had for one measure; it was of wheat, if they were of the richer sort; but of barley, if they were poorer. When these had so done, they shut themselves up in the inmost rooms of their houses, and ate the corn they had gotten; some did it without grinding it, by reason of the extremity of the want they were in, and others baked bread of it, according as necessity and fear dictated to them; a table was nowhere laid for a distinct meal, but they snatched the bread out of the fire, half baked, and ate it very hastily . . . The famine was too hard for all other passions,

and it is destructive to nothing so much as to modesty; for
what was otherwise worthy of reverence was in this case
despised; insomuch that children pulled the very morsels that
their fathers were eating out of their very mouths, and what
was still more to be pitied, so did the mothers do as to their
infants; and when those that were most dear were perishing
under their hands, they were not ashamed to take from them
the very last drops that might preserve their lives; and while
they ate after this manner, yet were they not concealed in so
doing; but the seditious everywhere came upon them immediately, and snatched away from them what they had gotten
from others; for when they saw any house shut up, this was
to them a signal that the people within had gotten some food;
whereupon they broke open the doors, and ran in, and took
pieces of what they were eating, almost up out of their very
throats, and this by force: the old men, who held their food
fast, were beaten; and if the women hid what they had within
their hands, their hair was torn for so doing; nor was there
any commiseration shown either to the aged or to infants;
. . . these tormentors were not themselves hungry; for the thing
had been less barbarous had necessity forced them to it; but
this was done to keep their madness in exercise."

"Titus sent a party of horsemen and ordered that they should
lay ambush for those that went out into the valleys to gather
food . . . the greater part of them were poor people, who were
deterred from deserting by the concern they were under for
their own relations . . . nor could they think of leaving these
relations to be slain by the robbers on their account; nay, the
severity of the famine made them bold in thus going out; so
nothing remained but that, when they were concealed from
the robbers, they should be taken by the enemy; and when
they were going to be taken, they were forced to defend themselves, for fear of being punished; as after they had fought,
they thought it too late to make any supplications for mercy;
so they were first whipped, and then tormented with all sorts

of tortures before they died, and were then crucified before the wall of the city. This miserable procedure made Titus greatly to pity them, while they caught every day five hundred Jews; nay, some days they caught more; yet did it not appear to be safe for him to let those taken by force go their way; and to set a guard over so many, he saw would be to make such as guarded them useless to him . . . So the soldiers, out of the wrath and hatred they bore the Jews, nailed those they caught, one after one way, and another after another, to the crosses, by way of jest; when their multitude was so great that room was wanting for the crosses, and crosses wanting for the bodies . . ."

"Now the seditious at first gave orders that the dead should be buried out of the public treasury, as not enduring the stench of their dead bodies. But afterwards, when they could not do that, they had them cast down from the walls into the valleys beneath. However, when Titus, in going his rounds along those valleys, saw them full of dead bodies, and the thick putrefaction running about them, he gave a groan; and spreading out his hands to heaven, called God to witness that this was not his doing . . . nor was there any place in the city that had no dead bodies in it, but what was entirely covered with those that were killed either by the famine or the rebellion. Now the number of those that were carried captive during this whole war was collected to be ninety-seven thousand; as was the number of those that perished in the whole siege eleven hundred thousand, the greater part of whom were indeed of the same nation (with the citizens of Jerusalem), but not belonging to the city itself; for they were come up from all the country to the feast of unleavened bread and were on a sudden shut up by an army . . . Accordingly the multitude of those that therein perished, exceeded all the destruction that either men or God ever brought upon the world . . . Yet did another plague seize upon those that were thus preserved, for the deserters used to swallow pieces of gold, but when this contrivance was discovered in one instance the fame of it filled their several camps, that the deserters came to them full of gold, so the multitude of the Arabians with the Syrians, cut up those who came as supplicants, and searched their inwards. Nor does it seem to me that any misery befell the Jews that was more terrible than this, since in one night's time about two thousand of these deserters were thus dissected."

These random quotations from the works of Josephus surely reveal the awful intensity of the tribulation. The followers of Christ escaped it because they complied with His commands and for their sakes the days of tribulation were shortened, for otherwise the siege of Jerusalem would have devastated the entire land. So completely were our Lord's words fulfilled when He said of the temple buildings, that not one stone should be left upon another that Josephus says, "If any one that had known the place before had come to it now, yet would he have inquired for it notwithstanding." So thoroughly did the Romans do their work that they even ploughed the spot whereon the temple stood. The axe, which John the Baptist saw at the root of the tree, had fallen, and very tragic was the stroke.

We now come to the remaining verses dealing with the fall of Jerusalem, and find the language becoming even stronger and more vivid. The description given in Matthew twenty-four, verses twenty-nine to thirty-four, could very easily be interpreted as applying to the last days and the Lord's return. We must, however, abide by our principle of ascertaining the true meaning of the terminology employed, and how the words are used in other parts of Scripture. Here our Lord says, "Immediately after the tribulation of those days shall the sun be darkened, and the moon shall not give her light, and the stars shall fall from heaven and the powers of heaven shall be shaken" (Matthew 24:29). Let us now search the Scriptures to see if at any other time such words have been used in predicting the downfall of a nation and the extinguishing of its light. If we turn to Isaiah 13:10, we find the prophet foretelling the downfall of Babylon and he makes his announcement in these strange words: "For the stars of heaven and the constellations thereof shall not give their light: The sun shall be darkened in his going forth, and the moon shall not cause her light to shine." In those words the prophet describes the extinction of a great nation. If we turn to Isaiah 34:4, we find the prophet describing the doom of Idumea in almost identical language: "All the host of heaven shall be dissolved, and the heaven shall be rolled together as a scroll: and all their host shall fall down, as the leaf falleth off from the vine, and as a falling fig from the figtree." Now everyone knows that this is pictorial language which did not have a literal fulfillment. If we insist on a literal interpretation of those passages, the infidel has ground for saying the prophet was mistaken. But the prophet was employing poetic language to describe the fall of a nation. The same language confronts us in Ezekiel 32:7 and 8 in which the prophet raises a lamentation for the fearful fall of the land of Egypt: "I will cover the sun with a cloud, and the moon shall not give her light. All the bright lights of heaven will I make dark over thee." We are especially interested in another such instance in the second chapter of the prophecy of Joel, verses 28 to 32. There God has promised the outpouring of His Spirit and follows that promise with the words, (verses 30, 31) "I will show wonders in the heavens and in the earth, blood, and fire, and pillars of smoke. The sun shall be turned into darkness, and the moon into blood, before the great and the terrible day of the Lord come." On the day of Pentecost, Peter explained that the outpouring of the Holy Spirit was the fulfillment of Joel's prophecy. The part referring to the sun and moon, however, was not fulfilled at Pentecost, but followed in logical sequence as promised, and was fulfilled at the destruction of Jerusalem. Believers in the Divine inspiration of Scripture are ready to admit that the Spirit which was upon the Anointed One was also the Spirit which inspired the Word. Surely, then, there is no reason why the Lord Jesus Christ should not use the terminology which He has put in the mouths of His holy prophets. This is exactly what He is doing in this instance. It was with some satisfaction that we made the discovery that the Greek New Testament gives these words as a quotation. Any reader can verify this by glancing at the reference to the sun, moon and stars, and the powers of heaven in Matthew twenty-four, verse twenty-nine. The heavy type used in the Greek makes it immediately evident to the eye that this is a quotation. Our Lord is quoting the language of the Old Testament. The Old Testament described nations under such figures, and the same method is adopted here. The sun did definitely set so far as Judaism was concerned.

The thirtieth verse of Matthew twenty-four describes the sign of the Son of man in heaven; the lamentation of the tribes of the earth, and the coming of the Son of man in the clouds of heaven in great power and great glory. What this sign was no one can say with any dogmatism. The arrangement of this passage of Scripture can easily lend itself to the interpretation that it was the Son of man who was in heaven, rather than the sign. This sign of the Son of man in heaven was simply the final culmination of the events prophesied on the Mount of Olives concerning Jerusalem. The Son of man was bringing to pass every incident which He had foretold, until the climax was reached which made all the tribes of the earth to mourn. The tribes mentioned here were, of course, the tribes of Israel. Much cause for mourning and lamentation had characterized their history, but this was their crowning sorrow and final desolation. This was the day of Jacob's trouble, as forseen by Jeremiah when he said, "Alas! for that day is great, so that none is like it: it is even the time of Jacob's trouble; but he shall be saved out of it" (Jeremiah 30:7). A remnant was saved out of it but many perished in the overthrow.

The next condition set forth is, "They shall see the Son of man coming in the clouds of heaven with power and great glory." It is not surprising that this clause is so generally accepted as referring to the Lord's return, for that seems to be its obvious meaning. It is, however, very easy for us to forget that some words are not used today with the meaning they had two thousand years ago. Our Lord Jesus Christ was familiar with the language of the Old Testament and frequently used its figures of speech. In the Old Testament a Divine visitation of a providential nature was frequently referred to as a coming of the Lord. In Genesis 11:5 we read, "the Lord came down to see the city." In Exodus 3:8, God says, "I am come down to deliver them." In Psalm 72:6 the Psalmist says, "He shall come down like rain upon the mown grass." Isaiah, showing the folly of looking to Egypt for help, says, "So shall the Lord of hosts come down to fight for Mount Zion, and for the hill thereof" (Isaiah 31:4). None of these passages suggests that God came in visible and personal form to dwell upon the earth at that time; neither is that suggested by Matthew 24:30. We take second place to no one in our conviction that the Lord will return personally and visibly, but we cannot blind ourselves to the fact that on this occasion He was using Old Testament figures of speech, which frequently described God as coming with clouds. The Lord said to Moses, "Lo, I come unto thee in a thick cloud" (Exodus 19:9). "The Lord descended in the cloud, and stood with him there" (Exodus 34:5). "Who maketh the clouds His chariot: who walketh upon the wings of the wind" (Psalm 104:3). Many other passages could be cited to show that Divine visitations were spoken of as the coming of the Lord in the clouds. "Clouds and darkness are round about Him" (Psalm 97:2). The words, "They shall see the Son of man coming in the clouds of heaven," do not present too much difficulty, for even to this day men speak of seeing God in some manifestation of His power. Those whose minds were spiritually enlightened could certainly see the Son of man in the clouds of heaven which came down so darkly upon Jerusalem at this time. Our former quotation from Dr. G. Campbell Morgan is more to the point in this connection. He says. "Some hold that the Second Advent of Jesus is past; that He actually came in Person at the time of the fall of Jerusalem; and was seen of some few faithful souls. There may be an element of truth in that view, but that does not exhaust the teaching of the New Testament concerning the Second Advent. He had often come before; He had talked with Abraham; He had spoken to men in the past as the Angel of Jehovah, AND WHO SHALL SAY THAT IN HIS PERSONAL FORM HE DID NOT GUIDE THE ROMAN LEGIONS AS THEY TOOK JERUSALEM?"[4] To some this statement might seem objectionable, yet it is certain that God is always present spiritually and providentially at every visitation of wrath upon men and nations from that day to this. It was not without some satisfaction to us, after having studied this chapter for some time, to make the discovery that Dr. Campbell Morgan, while not interpreting all the signs, says of Matthew twenty-four, "In verses five to thirty-five, the prophetic utterance concerned the excommunicated nation."[5]

It now remains for us only to mention the thirty-first verse of Matthew twenty-four, "And he shall send his angels with a great sound of trumpet, and they shall gather together his elect from the four winds, from one end of heaven to the other." We know that no Bible scholar will deny that the word, translated *angels* in this passage, is also translated *messengers* at least seven times in the New Testament, and in neither case does it apply to a celestial being. Three times the word is used of John the Baptist. In Luke 9:52 the term is applied to the disciples of Christ. In II Corinthians 12:7 the same word is used in describing the messenger of Satan that came to buffet the apostle Paul, while in James 2:25 it is used to designate the spies hidden by Rahab. In the book of Revelation, Jesus Christ commanded John to write to the angel of

(4)   Morgan, G. C., THE GOSPEL ACCORDING TO MATTHEW, Page 105-6
(5)   Morgan, G. C., THE GOSPEL ACCORDING TO MATTHEW, Page 284

each of the seven churches in Asia, but our Lord was not dictating letters to the angels who do His will and behold His face, but to the ministers of the seven churches in Asia Minor. Christ's ministers and messengers were therefore the *angelous* or *angels* commissioned to gather His elect from the four winds of heavens by the preaching of the gospel. This world-wide mission, which really began with the destruction of Jerusalem, removed the shackles of Judaism and formally brought to an end the old dispensation. The blowing of the great trumpet is also a figurative expression. The metaphor abounds in Scripture in connection with such important pronouncements as the day of Jubilee and other similar occasions. The messengers of Christ were now to go forth in His name, heralding the day of Jubilee for as many as should believe the Gospel.

The foregoing thoughts have led us to the conviction that while tribulation may be the portion of God's people in this world, and while that tribulation may be intensified as apostasy increases, yet the Great Tribulation of Daniel's prophecy and of Matthew twenty-four took place at the destruction of Jerusalem, thereby fulfilling our Lord's prophecy that it should happen within that generation. That was the time of Jacob's trouble, and of the natural Israel's travail and sorrow. It is not without significance that none of the gospel writers ever refers to any other Great Tribulation; neither is there any mentioned in the New Testament Epistles.

It is but fitting that we should bring in one further illustration of how the word of the Lord was magnified and fulfilled in the destruction of Jerusalem. Josephus tells the story of a wealthy and cultured woman who was robbed of all her possessions during the siege, and we quote his words: "She slew her infant son, and then roasted him, and ate the one half of him, and kept the other half by her concealed. Upon this the seditious came in presently, and smelling the horrid scent of this food, they threatened her that they would cut her throat immediately if she did not show them what food she had gotten ready. She replied that she had saved a very fine portion of it for them, and withal uncovered what was left of her son. Hereupon they were seized with a horror and amazement of mind, and stood astonished at the sight, when she said to them, 'This is mine own son, and what hath been done was mine own doing! Come, eat of this food; for I have eaten of it myself. Do not you pretend to be either more tender than a woman, or more compassionate than a mother; but if you be so scrupulous and do abominate this my sacrifice, as I have eaten the one half, let the rest be reserved for me also!' After which those men went out trembling, being never so much affrighted at any thing as they were at this, and with some difficulty they left the rest of that meat to the mother." Having quoted these words of a secular historian, we now wish to quote the prophecy which that incident fulfilled: "The Lord shall bring a nation against thee from afar, from the end of the earth, as swift as the eagle flieth; a nation whose tongue thou shalt not understand; . . . And he shall besiege thee in all thy gates, until thy high and fenced walls come down, wherein thou trustedst, throughout all thy land; and he shall besiege thee in all thy gates throughout all thy land, which the Lord thy God hath given thee. And thou shalt eat the fruit of thine own body, the flesh of thy sons and of thy daughters, which the Lord thy God hath given thee, in the siege, and in the straitness, wherewith thine enemies shall distress thee; So that the man that is tender among you, and very delicate, his eye shall be evil toward his brother, and toward the wife of his bosom, and toward the remnant of his children which he shall leave: So that he will not give to any of them of the flesh of his children whom he shall eat: because he hath nothing left him in the siege, and in the straitness, wherewith thine enemies shall distress thee in all thy gates. The tender and delicate woman among you, which would not adventure to set the sole of her foot upon the ground for delicateness and tenderness, her eye shall be evil toward the husband of her bosom, and toward her son, and toward her daughter, and toward her young one that cometh out from between her feet, and toward her children which she shall bear: for she shall eat them for want of all things secretly in the siege and straitness, wherewith thine enemy shall distrees thee in thy gates" (Deuteronomy 28:49, 52-57). As we behold all this evidence of God's faithfulness to His word, it is something to fill our souls with awe and adoring reverence. It is a far cry from Moses to Josephus; yet that which was promised by God through Moses, His ambassador, is recorded as having its fulfillment by a historian, who without regard to what God had promised, faithfully reports what God has done.

It has been necessary to write this lengthy chapter dealing with the teachings of Matthew twenty-four and therefore space will permit but a passing reference to some of the other passages in which dispensationalists find the tribulation of the end-time, which presumably will take place after the rapture and resurrection of the saints. The prophet Daniel places the resurrection of both saints and sinners after the tribulation and this fact should militate against dispensational teachings which insist that the contrary is the case.

It is also held that the second Psalm teaches the Great Tribulation where it says, "Then shall he speak to them in his wrath and vex them in his sore displeasure" (Psalm 2:5). This is interpreted as taking place previous to the setting of the King upon the holy hill of Zion. It is all so plain (to the dispensationalist) that Jehovah's speaking in wrath is the Great Tribulation, which takes place before the setting up of the kingdom. All that need be said of this is that one who finds the Great Tribulation in the second Psalm can find it anywhere. Where in Scripture does the wrath of God mean the Great Tribulation? In First Thessalonians 1:10 Paul reminds the Thessalonians that Jesus saved them "from the wrath to come." Will any one insist that this means they were saved from the Great Tribulation, which is supposed to occur thousands of years later? When John the Baptist asked the Pharisees and Sadducees, "Who hath warned you to flee from the wrath to come?" he could not have referred to the Great Tribulation. The apostle Paul, writing to the Romans, said, "The wrath of God is revealed from heaven against all ungodliness and unrighteousness of men" (Romans 1:18). Paul did not surely mean that at that time they were in the Great Tribulation! Dispensationalists would hardly interpret that passage to say so.

The wrath of God is plainly revealed to be something other than the Great Tribulation by many parts of Scripture. An example of this may be found in John 3:36: "He that believeth on the Son hath everlasting life: and he that believeth not the Son shall not see life; but the wrath of God abideth on him." We leave it to the reader to decide whether "the wrath of God" in this passage has any relation to the Great Tribulation. Paul, writing to the Ephesians, reminds them that they were "by nature children of wrath, even as others" (Ephesians 2:3). Does this mean that they were by nature heirs of the Great Tribulation? In his letter to the Colossians, Paul writes that because of certain things, "the wrath of God cometh on the children of disobedience" (Colossians 3:6). Millions of people have died in their sins with the wrath of God upon them but that did not mean they had passed, or should pass, through this Great Tribulation. Surely our fellow-Christians, who build a doctrine on so flimsy a foundation, must be aware of all this, for it is plain to any reader of the Bible.

We have recently talked with a brother minister who is convinced that the Great Tribulation is still in the future, and quotes in support of his belief the message of our Lord to the church in Philadelphia, as recorded in Revelation 3:10, "Because thou hast kept the word of my patience, I also will keep thee from the hour of temptation, which shall come upon all the world, to try them that dwell upon the earth." Our brother contended that this was written after the destruction of Jerusalem and must therefore refer to the tribulation of the future. Our answer to this argument is that most people know that the seven churches of Asia, including Philadelphia, were not mythical, or figurative, but historical realities. In that case the message to the church in Philadelphia had its primary application to that church, while it may also be edifying to us. This is true, for example, of the Epistles to the Corinthians, and Galatians. Their primary application was to the particular churches to which they were originally addressed, but they are edifying to the people of God until the end of time. God gave the members of the Philadelphian church certain promises, among them that of deliverance from a universal temptation. Every one knows that all the members of that Philadelphian church have long since left this earth. If God fulfilled His promise to them, then the "temptation" must have occurred in their day. If this promise refers to a future tribulation, how can it apply to people dead and gone two thousand years? How can it have any fulfillment in their experience? As a matter of fact the "temptation" mentioned in Revelation 3:10 is not necessarily related to any tribulation. The word used is *Peirasmos* which means *trial, proving,* or *testing.* It is the same word which is used in the Lord's Prayer, "Lead us not into temptation." We have not heard dispensationalists say that the Lord's Prayer asks for deliverance from the Great Tribulation. Every experienced Christian knows that temptation is the universal experience of all the children of God, but "the Lord knoweth how to deliver the godly out of temptation" (II Peter 2:9). Here again the same term is used. This was the promise that God gave to the church at Philadelphia a promise which He doubtless fulfilled. We are compelled, in all honesty, to say that from a careful study of those passages upon which this theory is so painstakingly built up, we have not found one passage in the entire Bible that is capable of only this interpretation, i.e., that the Great Tribulation of Daniel's prophecy and of Matthew twenty-four is still future. We have read all the writings on this subject to which we had access, and have not found one absolutely convincing argument in its favor. We are, therefore, satisfied to believe that the tribulation here prophesied actually took place in 70 A. D. until such time as concrete and convincing Scriptural evidence to the contrary is offered. We believe dispensationalism has already explored every avenue offering any possibility of this with results disappointing to itself and not convincing to others.

For the sake of better understanding, it might be plainly stated that we do not deny that there shall be great tribulation toward the end of the Gospel age. Those who have spiritual discernment can already hear the rumblings which betoken the loosening of an avalanche of apostasy. As it gains momentum, life will become increasingly difficult for those who remain steadfast in the faith, and loyal to Jesus Christ. Some of them are already paying a price for their devotion to Him.

The professing church is gradually, but surely, concentrating its endeavors on carnal organization which shall presumably embrace all of Christendom. The indications of ecclesiastical regimentation are everywhere in evidence. The question of questions is whether the world organization shall be under the direction of Christ, or of Antichrist. The history of ecclesiastical mergers does not justify the hope of world revival under a world church. The alternative is world-wide apostasy.

As the suffering of God's people is intensified, and as the ostracism and the persecution become more obvious, let the redeemed of the Lord lift up their heads, for their salvation drawth nigh. He Who said, "In this world ye shall have tribulation," also said, "Be of good cheer, I have overcome the world."

Chapter 10.

The Rapture

IT HAS been the age-old belief of the Christian church that God has, in His own eternal councils, appointed a day in which He shall bring the members of the human race before His judgment seat to be assigned to their eternal destinies. This belief is amply supported by the Holy Scriptures which speak of the Lord's return, the resurrection of the dead, and the final judgment, as simultaneous events. This is also suggested by the Apostles' Creed which speaks of Christ's return, and the judgment of the quick and the dead, in the same clause. In Scripture, and elsewhere, the time when this series of events shall take place is described as "the day of the Lord," or "the day of Christ."

Dispensationalism insists that these two designations do not mean the same thing; but that they refer to two events, separated by seven years of time. Every one who is familiar with dispensational literature has read the hackneyed phrase, "two phases of the same event." It is a matter of necessity that dispensationalism should have the event divided into two phases in order to agree with the intricate system of which these "two phases" are such important parts. The "two phases" receive no support from Scripture, but it is necessary to give Scripture this interpretation in order to shore up a structure which is uncomfortably shaky. The unfortunate misplacing of the seventieth week of Daniel's prophecy, and of relegating the Great Tribulation promised by Daniel to the seven years immediately preceding the Lord's return, has invested the beautiful orderliness of Scripture with manifest confusion. The promise given to the disciples of Christ that they should escape this tribulation which culminated in the destruction of Jerusalem (a promise which has been literally fulfilled), is interpreted to mean that the church of Christ shall be raptured out of the world before the tribulation of the end-time. It is a fact universally known that one error needs to be supported by another, and then another, until there is an endless chain of confusing and contradictory statements. A theological error is no exception to this rule. The consequence of this particular error is a bewildering plurality of returns of Christ, of resurrections, and judgments such as were never known to the Apostolic or the Reformation Church. This observation is made not churlishly or critically, for dispensationalists themselves frankly admit that some of their doctrines were not known to either the Church Fathers or the Reformers. One of the leading men of this school, writing of the theory that the church was a mystery first revealed to Paul, has this to say, "In fact, until brought to the fore through the writings and the preaching of a distinguished ex-clergyman, Mr. J. N. Darby, in the early part of last century, it is scarcely to be found in a single book or sermon throughout a period of 1600 years! If any doubt this statement, let them search, as the writer has in a measure done, the remarks of the so-called Fathers both pre- and post-Nicene, the theological treatises of the scholastic divines, Roman Catholic writers of all shades of thought; the literature of the Reformation; the sermons and the expositions of the Puritans and the theological works of the day, he will find the 'mystery' conspicuous by its absence."[1] This gentleman is absolutely right, and the same thing could be said of so many things, "brought to the fore by the writings and preaching of Mr. J. N. Darby in the early part of the last century."

We now address ourselves particularly to a consideration of the event which will, we believe, bring to an end this dispensation and usher in that "everlasting kingdom which shall never be destroyed," namely, the return of our Lord from heaven. Dispensationalism teaches that the first concomitant of this event will be the secret rapture of the church. It is held that

---

(1) Ironside, Harry A., MYSTERIES OF GOD, Page 50

our Lord will come part way and be met in the air by His resurrected and raptured saints, and that they will remain with Him at this rendezvous for a period of seven years. This first phase of the Lord's return is known as the Rapture, while the second and final phase is known as the Revelation. The first phase is presumably derived from the Greek word *parousia,* while the second phase is based upon the Greek word *apokalupsis.*

It is to the word *parousia* that we wish to give our attention in this chapter. We believe that properly understood, the *parousia* (*coming*) and the *apocalupsis* (*revelation*) shall be seen as simultaneous events. Nothing in the word of God proves that there will be seven years between the *parousia* and the *apocalupsis.* Let us look at the New Testament passages in which this word *parousia* appears. In I Corinthians 15:23 we read the words, "Christ the first fruits; afterward they that are Christ's at his (*parousia*) coming." In I Thessalonians 2:19 we read the words, "For what is our hope, or joy, or crown of rejoicing? Are not even ye in the presence of our Lord Jesus Christ at His (*parousia*) coming." The same translation is made in I Thessalonians 3:13, I Thessalonians 4:15, I Thessalonians 5:23, and II Thessalonians 2:1. If the word *parousia* does not actually mean *coming* then the translators of the Bible up to this day have been guilty of a serious overstatement and disservice. If it does not mean *coming,* how can it be interpreted to mean "coming part of the way?"

The Rev. Alexander Reese, himself a premillennialist, has written an excellent book called, *The Approaching Advent of Christ* in which he devotes an entire chapter to this word *parousia.* Mr. Reese quotes the following words from Deissmann's *Light from the Ancient East.* " 'From the Ptolemaic period down into the second century we are able to trace the word in the east as a technical expression for the arrival or visit of the king or emperor, (or other persons in authority, or troops). The parousia of the sovereign must have been something well known even to the people as shown by the facts that special payments in kind and taxes to defray the cost of the parousia were exacted, that in Greece a new era was reckoned from the parousia of the Emperor Hadrian, that all over the world advent coins were struck after a parousia of the emperor and that we are even able to quote examples of advent sacrifices.'[2] The early Christians knew very well what was involved in the parousia of the emperor. They too had a king-emperor whom they expected to come and they were making preparation for His parousia. Dr. James Moffat has a short article on the word *parousia* in *Hasting's Encyclopaedia of Religion and Ethics,* Volume 9, Page 637, in which we read the following: 'On the lips of the Greek-speaking Christians in the primitive church *parousia* was almost exclusively applied to the return of Christ in glory in order to complete the Messianic work and usher in the Final Judgment.' This same article contains a quotation from Milligan's *St. Paul's Epistle to the Thessalonians* in which it says, 'The Greek word meant both *arrival* and *presence* and in the papyri it denotes especially the visit of an official or monarch.' "

We can well imagine the thoughts passing through the minds of those suffering Christians in the early church as they read in Paul's letters of the *parousia* of their Lord. They probably witnessed the *parousia* of a Roman emperor with all its pomp, and its tokens and trophies of conquest. There was a *parousia* yet to come in which they were to be given signal recognition and in the joys of which they were to participate. It is, however, difficult to see how the theory of a "secret coming," and that only "part of the way" could be based upon the word *parousia,* the *arrival of the king.* This unwarranted twisting of Scripture can hardly be expected to further the interests of truth. Truth does not have to be supported by error.

There are many Christian people who feel that to surrender this theory of spending seven years in mid-air with Christ

---

(2) Reese, Alexander, THE APPROACHING ADVENT OF CHRIST, Page 143

would necessarily deprive them of the Rapture, which they plainly see in Scripture, and also the escape from the Great Tribulation, which seems so desirable. We have already shown that the Great Tribulation of prophecy is past. We shall not experience that one, although we may have other tribulations. As for the Rapture, every Christian living or dead at the Lord's return will participate in it. This is not difficult to understand if we read out of Scripture what the Holy Spirit has written into it, instead of seeking confirmation for our own preconceived notions. The Rapture is plainly taught in the Word of God. In I Thessalonians 4:17 we read of the Lord's coming when the saints who are alive shall be caught up, and in company with their fellow-believers of all the ages, resurrected from the dead, shall "meet the Lord in the air." Now, surely, this passage does not say that they are to remain where they meet for seven years. This idea is without the slightest support from Scripture. In Matthew 25 our Lord discussed His own return and the Rapture of the church in these words, "Then shall the kingdom of heaven be likened unto ten virgins, which took their lamps, and went forth to meet the bridegroom" (Matthew 25:1). Both wise and foolish virgins heard the midnight cry, and stirred themselves up to go out and meet the coming bridegroom. It was then that their unreadiness became known to the foolish virgins. The wise went out joyously to meet him, and returned with him. It is scarcely necessary to point out that there is not the slightest suggestion of their having remained where they met for seven years. The bridegroom had come part of the way when they met him and he continued his journey to pronounce immediate judgment upon the unready and foolish virgins, and to celebrate the marriage supper with his own.

We now come to give our attention to the nature of the Rapture, which this new school of thought tells us will take place in absolute secrecy. The human mind has given full rein to its imaginative powers in this realm. Those who have read the little tract, *Missing,* know what an unforgettable picture it presented of a world suddenly finding itself bereft of every Christian man and woman. Industries and utilities are immobilized, families are separated, children are crying for mothers and fathers who cannot be found. Husbands look for their wives, and wives for their husbands, not knowing whither the raptured ones have gone. The most recent presentation of this sacriligious and unscriptural view has found its expression in a movie film depicting the world's confusion after the Rapture. It is reported that many are converted through the message of this picture. Doubtless many are frightened but we seriously question whether the Spirit of God condescends to bless error and falsehood to the salvation of souls. These words of ours are not too strong a characterization of this doctrine, which is so destitute of Scriptural support, that many dispensationalists feel compelled to abandon it. Rev. Alexander Reese, a premillennialist, calls it a "dangerous delusion" and says, "Men who taught this dangerous delusion were capable of teaching other beautiful and comforting errors on the Second Coming. And they did; and did it with such a success that multitudes in all the churches hail them as heaven-sent truths worth dying for."[3]

Let us now consider a few of the outstanding passages which are said to teach the "Secret Rapture." The familiar dispensational stronghold for this theory is I Thessalonians 4:15-17: "For this we say unto you by the word of the Lord, that we which are alive and remain unto the coming of the Lord shall not prevent them which are asleep. For the Lord himself shall descend from heaven with a shout, with the voice of the archangel, and with the trump of God: and the dead in Christ shall rise first: Then we which are alive and remain shall be caught up together with them in the clouds, to meet the Lord in the air: and so shall we ever be with the Lord." The apostle Paul was comforting the Thessalonian believers concerning their Christian brethren who had passed on. He tells the Thes-

---

(3) Reese, Alexander, THE APPROACHING ADVENT OF CHRIST, Page 148

salonians that not only the living, but also the dead, will be caught up to meet the Lord in the air at His coming. The raptured and ressurected saints will go up together to meet Him. But where is there any word here about a *silent* or *secret* rapture? Alexander Reese, speaking of this theory, says, "The suggestion of Darby, backed by the vigorous efforts of Kelly and others, to prove from this magnificent passage in I Thessalonians 4, that a secret coming, a resurrection, and a secret rapture, are portrayed, followed by the rise and reign of the Antichrist, is among the sorriest in the whole history of freak exegesis."[4] The event leading to the Rapture of the church and the resurrection of the dead is "The Lord himself will descend from heaven with a shout"; (Is that secret?) "With the voice of the archangel"; (Is that secret?) "and with the trump of God." If any one can interpret that to mean something secret, it is because language is robbed of its meaning. We pass on to our readers at this point a rather amusing incident reported by the late Dr. Rowland Bingham, at one time editor of the *Evangelical Christian,* and General Director of the Sudan Interior Mission, in his book, *Mathew the Publican and His Gospel*: "My wife set the investigating machinery going one day by saying, 'Rowland, where do you get the *Secret Rapture* idea in the Bible? I have to teach the Second Coming to my class of young women on Sunday and I have been hunting for some proof of the Secret Rapture.' I quite glibly replied, 'First Thessalonians four.' 'But,' she said, 'I have been reading that and it is about the noisiest thing in my Bible. *The Lord shall descend from heaven with a shout, with the voice of the archangel and the trump of God . . .'* I tried a second thrust by suggesting that there was the type of Enoch being secretly translated while Noah went through the judgment, to which there came the counter blow that knocked me out of the ring as she said, 'You know, Rowland, that you cannot build a doctrine on a type.' Later I said to my unsatisfied wife, 'My

---

(4) Reese, Alexander, THE APPROACHING ADVENT OF CHRIST, Page 146

teachers all affirmed that the Greek very clearly differentiates between the Secret Rapture of the church and the public manifestation to the world. The word *parousia* always indicates the rapture, while *epiphaneia* always has to do with the appearing of Christ with His Church . . .' But that help-meet of mine wanted to do what I had never done, check up on these two Greek words: And so there was nothing for it but to get out my *Young's Concordance* and turn up every text in which the word *parousia* appeared. It smashed the theory of the Secret Rapture so hopelessly that I marvelled at the credulity with which I had swallowed my 'Authorities.' " It is a pity that there are not more Bible students with this discernment, for then many baseless theories would not find such ready acceptance.

Dr. S. P. Tregelles, an eminent Greek scholar, writing on this subject in 1864 says, "I am not aware that there was any definite teaching that there should be a Secret Rapture of the Church at a secret coming until this was given forth as an 'utterance' in Mr. Irving's church from what was then received as being the voice of the Spirit. But whether anyone ever asserted such a thing or not it was from that supposed revelation that the modern doctrine and the modern phraseology respecting it arose. It came, not from Holy Scripture, but from that which falsely pretended to be the Spirit of God, while not owning the true doctrine of our Lord's incarnation in the same flesh and blood as His brethren, but without taint of sin."[5] If it be said that the theory of the Secret Rapture has been and is now held by great and good men, it can also be said that many great and good men failed to find it in Scripture. Luther, Calvin, Knox, Wesley, Whitfield, and Spurgeon, and a host of others could not be accused of shutting their eyes to the teachings of God's Word, yet nowhere in their writings can one find the slightest suggestion of a belief in a Secret Rapture. I Thessalonians 4 certainly does not teach it, but quite the contrary.

---

(5) Tregelles, S. P., THE HOPE OF CHRIST'S SECOND COMING, Page 35

Dr. T. T. Shields, a great expositor of Scripture, says, "There is nothing in Scripture to suggest that the dead will rise amid a great silence . . . Surely you will not say that the trumpet, by any stretch of the imagination, can be intended to mean some secret procedure. The very idea of 'the shout,' 'the voice of the archangel,' and 'the trump of God' proclaims an audible public event. And that is what the Bible says about the coming of Christ. I cannot find, then, in this specific Scripture (I Thessalonians 4:13-18) any authority for the Secret Rapture of the saints. I am myself persuaded that there is not one shred of Scripture anywhere to support this theory. I am sure that it is a figment of the human imagination."[6]

The Secret Rapture is sometimes argued from the statement that "The day of the Lord cometh as a thief in the night." But it is the day that comes as a thief in the night when least expected. The Lord does not come as a thief taking advantage of the darkness to carry off what does not belong to Him. Some modern "Young Lochinvars" have found it necessary to elope because of objections to the marriage. The Lord Jesus Christ shall not be under any such obligation. He shall take to Himself His blood-bought bride before a startled universe. He uses the simile of a thief in the night, simply to warn men that His coming will find great numbers off their guard and not expecting Him. "If the goodman of the house had known in what watch the thief would come, he would have watched" (Matthew 24:43).

The Christian church has traditionally believed that our Lord's frequent statements concerning the surprising and startling nature of His return are to be interpreted as admonitions to the church to continue without flagging her work of directing sinners to Christ for salvation, inasmuch as the Lord's return will mark the end of all opportunity to flee from the wrath to come. The idea that there shall be a great religious revival among those left behind, when the church is raptured,

---

(6)   Shields, T. T., THE GOSPEL WITNESS, Sept. 26, 1935

is quite a modern invention. The Scriptures teach implicitly and explicitly that the Lord's return, the Rapture of the church, and the resurrection of the dead will take place at one and the same time, and will mark the end forever of all opportunity of salvation.

If we take the departure of the wise virgins to meet the coming bridegroom as an analogy of the Rapture of the church, it seems to prove conclusively that not even penitent and pleading sinners were any longer accepted by Jesus Christ. The apostle Peter, answering the scoffers who doubted the truth of the Lord's return, tells them to consider the Lord's long-suffering for their salvation. The Lord was delaying His coming because He was unwilling that any should perish. Dr. Shields, commenting on this, speaks as follows: "Peter plainly teaches that the period of grace, the dispensation of grace, will end with the coming of Jesus Christ. There will not be millions saved after the Lord comes. I can find no such teaching in the New Testament. Indeed, He will come, 'In flaming fire taking vengeance on them that know not God' — and what else? — 'and that obey not the gospel of our Lord Jesus Christ.' Why will he come? To take vengeance 'on them that obey not the gospel of our Lord Jesus Christ' — not to give them another chance to repent and believe it. My brethren, 'behold, now is the accepted time; behold, now is the day of salvation.' I do not know when the Lord will come, but I do know — I am sure of it, for myself, as of my own existence — that when at last Jesus Christ comes down from the skies, when that lightning flash shall sweep across the heavens, and the world shall be startled with the shout, and with the voice of the archangel, and the trump of God; when that takes place, the doom of every unrepentant soul will be forever settled; the day of grace will be over; the day of judgment will be ushered in."[7]

This does not agree with the theory put forth by dispensationalism to the effect that after the church is raptured and the

(7) Shields, T. T., THE GOSPEL WITNESS, Jan. 25, 1940

Holy Spirit is taken away, the earth will witness a great religious revival as a result of Gospel preaching by the Jewish remnant. Dr. Oswald Allis in his book, *Prophecy and the Church,* reproduces on page 282 an advertisement used extensively by the American Board of Missions to the Jews, under the caption, "Who Will Preach the Gospel When the Church Is Gone?" The advertisement answers this question in the words, "If you are a well-taught child of God you know the answer — the Jews — of course. We sometimes call them Tribulation Jews. To them we must hand our torch of witness that they may carry on after we have heard the shout from heaven."[8] Dr. Allis asks a question in this connection which dispensationalism does not answer, and that is, why are Christian Jews to be left behind after the church is taken away? We are asked at present to contribute our money for the conversion of the Jews, so that when the church is raptured, they shall preach the Gospel during the tribulation. This offers a conundrum to anyone willing to think it through. If the Jews are converted, are they not converted to Christ? Are they not then the members of the body of Christ, which is His church? Will an incomplete body be His at the Rapture? We do not believe that any such doctrine is taught in the Word of God. If this is a definite teaching of Scripture we confess our inability to find it. Moreover, we think it nothing short of a dangerous and false hope to suggest to anyone the possibility of being saved after the church has been taken away. It is also a complicated problem to show by what agency sinners among Jews or Gentiles can be converted after the Holy Spirit has been withdrawn from the earth. Every Christian minister and evangelist will readily acknowledge his inability to convert a sinner to Christ apart from the power of the Holy Spirit, and has found the *Westminster Shorter Catechism* to be true to experience where it says, "The Spirit of God maketh the reading, but especially the preaching of the Word, an effectual means of

(8) Allis, Oswald, PROPHECY AND THE CHURCH, Page 282

convincing and converting sinners, and of building them up in holiness through faith unto salvation." An attempt is made to explain the conversion of sinners after the Holy Spirit is withdrawn by pointing out that the Old Testament saints were in possession of the Spirit of God centuries before the dispensation of the Spirit was inaugurated on the day of Pentecost and that in like manner men shall possess that Spirit after the dispensation of the Spirit has come to an end. The latter part of this explanation is without support from any plain, unmistakable utterance in the Word of God.

There is no plain teaching in the Bible to show that the church of God will be raptured secretly, but much plain teaching to the contrary. There is no plain teaching in the Bible to prove that there will be seven years of unparalleled tribulation between the Rapture of the church and the Lord's return to earth. This imaginary seven-year period owes its place in dispensational theology to the unscriptural separation of the seventieth week of Daniel's prophecy from the other sixty-nine weeks. It had to be inserted somewhere. There is, furthermore, no Scriptural support for the amazing theory that after the rapture of the church the Jews will carry on a vigorous evangelism by which many shall be saved. Let no one be deceived into thinking so, for "behold, now is the accepted time; behold, now is the day of salvation."

Let us listen to Peter as by Divine inspiration he describes the Lord's return in the third chapter of his second Epistle: "The day of the Lord shall come as a thief in the night" (verse 10). It shall come when it is least expected, and without any advance notice, other than we have already received. But shall it be a secret coming? The answer is here: "The heavens shall pass away with A GREAT NOISE" (verse 10). The dispensationalist says this shall be His coming *with* His saints, and not His coming *for* them. What does Peter say? "Wherefore, beloved, seeing that ye look for such things, be diligent that ye may be found of Him in peace, without spot, and blameless"

(II Peter 3:14). Peter teaches that "the day of the Lord" will find some of the saints here on earth. The day of vengeance found Lot in Sodom, but he was taken out of the overthrow to a place of safety as the fire began to fall. Let it be remembered that there was no revival in Sodom after Lot was taken out. No one was saved after that. No one was saved after Noah went into the ark and the flood came. Our Lord Himself, Who in His preincarnation form watched those conflagrations, has significantly stated that it shall be so at the coming of the Son of man.

Chapter 11.

The Resurrection

THE Apostles' Creed, recited by both Romanist and Protestant, includes among its articles of faith, a belief in the resurrection of the body. Beyond a bare professed acceptance of this phase of the Christian hope, it does not enter into any details. This doctrine featured largely in the faith of the earthly church, and was a powerful factor in its hope and endurance. The resurrection of Jesus Christ from the dead was regarded as the final and all-sufficient proof of the resurrection of all mankind. As the human race inherited the tragic legacy of death through the first Adam, so the last Adam was to nullify the tragedy by the abolition of the last enemy — death. "For as in Adam all die, even so in Christ shall all be made alive" (I Corinthians 15:22). It does not come within the scope of this work to enter into a critical examination of the doctrine of the resurrection; but rather to aim at a clarification of a doctrine already wholeheartedly accepted as factual, "I believe in the resurrection of the body."

One of the questions treated by the apostle Paul in his first letter to the Corinthians was, "How are the dead raised up? and with what body do they come?" (I Corinthians 15:35). Our question in this chapter is, When are the dead raised up and in what order do they come? The *Westminster Confession of Faith* affirms that, "At the last day such as are found alive shall not die, but be changed; and all the dead shall be raised up with the self-same bodies and none other, although with different qualities, which shall be united again to their souls forever. The bodies of the unjust shall by the power of Christ be raised to dishonour; the bodies of the just by His Spirit unto honour, and be made conformable to His own glorious body."[1] We note particularly that the Confession states that all this will happen "at the last day."

Modern dispensationalism greatly disagrees with this affirmation, believing that there shall be at least three separate occasions in the future when great numbers of the dead shall be raised up. The first of these occasions is to be when the Lord shall come for His church. As the living saints are being raptured to meet the Lord in the air, the dead in Christ shall be raised up to ascend with them. While this multitude is participating in the "Marriage Supper of the Lamb" for seven years, the Jews are to be carrying on a vigorous evangelism on earth, converting many Gentiles. It will be remembered that, according to dispensationalism, this is the time of the Great Tribulation. The church will be gone and the Holy Spirit will have been withdrawn, but conversions are to be numerous. Some of the converts are to lay down their lives as the result of persecution by the Antichrist. At the close of the seven years, when the Lord shall come with His church, there is to be a resurrection of those "Tribulation Saints." These are to enter the millennium with those already resurrected. One thousand years later, there is to be a resurrection of those who have died Christless. They shall be raised up for the final judgment, which is to take place at the close of the millennial period.

There is not too much reason why the Christian should be greatly exercised over the question of whether his resurrection shall be in keeping with either one or the other of these plans. Our chief interest in making this investigation is to discover for ourselves which of those interpretations is true, for obviously they cannot both be true. One theory places the resurrection of all mankind at the last day, while the other insists that it shall take place in three distinct stages covering a period of one thousand and seven years. Paradoxically enough, each of these conflicting schools of thought quotes Scripture to prove the orthodoxy of its position. This is not so unusual as to cause any great surprise.

---

(1) Westminster Confession of Faith, Chapter XXXII

The first clear, unequivocal announcement of the resurrection of the just and the unjust is found in the twelfth chapter of the book of Daniel: "And many of them that sleep in the dust of the earth shall awake, some to everlasting life and some to shame and everlasting contempt" (Daniel 12:2). Both Christian and Jewish expositors regard this passage as a clear statement of the resurrection of the dead. S. P. Tregelles asks, "If the language of this passage be not declaratory of a resurrection of the dead, actual and literal, is there any passage of Scripture at all which speaks of such a thing as a resurrection?"[2] His question is to the point, in view of the interpretation given to this passage in more recent times.

Readers of the Scofield Reference Bible may be surprised at the scant consideration which it gives to this great passage. All the notice which it receives is the one word "resurrection" in fine print on the margin. The reason for this is not far to seek. Dr. A. C. Gaebelein, one of the consulting editors of the Scofield Reference Bible, denies that any resurrection is meant here. "Physical resurrection," says Dr. Gaebelein, "is not taught in the second verse of this chapter; if it were the passage would be in clash with the revelation concerning resurrection in the New Testament. There is no general resurrection, but there will be the first resurrection in which only the righteous participate, and the second resurrection which means the raising of the wicked dead for their eternal and conscious punishment. Between the two resurrections is a space of 1000 years. We repeat the passage has nothing to do with physical resurrection. Physical resurrection is, however, used as a figure of the national revival of Israel in that day. They have been sleeping nationally in the dust of the earth, buried among the Gentiles. But at that time there will take place a national restoration."[3] There is not any clash between this passage and "the revelation concerning resurrection in the New Testament." The clash is between the passage and Dr. Gaebelein's interpre-

(2)   Tregelles, S. P., on DANIEL, Page 168
(3)   Gaebelein, A. C., DANIEL, Page 200

tation of the revelation of the New Testament. It happens that Daniel places the tribulation before any resurrection, and that Daniel knows of no period of a thousand years' duration between the resurrection of the righteous and that of the wicked. For these reasons Dr. Gaebelein denies that Daniel is speaking of a physical resurrection. Commenting on these views of Dr. Gaebelein and William Kelly, Alexander Reese says, " And these are the men who condemn the spiritualizing of Old Testament prophecies, and tell us how unpardonable is the fault of those who explain away the first resurrection in Revelation 20:4. Yet they themselves, when their theories require it, are free to adopt the mischievous canon that they condemn in others. It is pitiable that whilst modern critical scholars are unanimous in insisting on the literal and miraculous character of the resurrection in Daniel 12:2 the theorists join hands with Sadducees and rationalists in reducing it to thin air."[4]

The twelfth chapter of Daniel has not only placed the resurrection of the just and the unjust at the same time, but it also involves another difficulty for the dispensationalist. It has placed the Tribulation before any resurrection. As a matter of fact, the twelfth chapter of Daniel is a conclusion which seems to summarize an entire dispensation. It speaks of an unparalleled tribulation for Daniel's people. But the resurrection does not necessarily follow immediately. "The resurrection," says Dr. W. M. Taylor, "is mentioned as a great fact which is to come at the close of all human history, and from it both warning and encouragement are drawn appropriate to the emergency of that dreadful time."[5] On the same page Dr. Taylor quotes the words of Carl August Auberlen as follows: "We have here a parallel to the epistles to the Seven Churches in the Revelation of John, which contain promises for those who overcome, and threats for those who fall away. The sole purpose for which the resurrection is introduced is to show the

(4)   Reese, Alexander, THE APPROACHING ADVENT OF CHRIST, Page 42

(5)   Taylor, W. M., DANIEL THE PROPHET, Page 209

causal connection between the behaviour of the people during the time of their probation and their eternal state; but not the slightest intimation is given as to the chronological relation between the time of distress and that of resurrection."

In the light of these observations we are justified in concluding that Daniel 12:2 teaches a general resurrection at the end of the age. It has been pointed out to us that Daniel's mention of the just and the unjust in itself implies the two resurrections. This argument has little merit for, by the same token, if Daniel had said that there would be a resurrection of white and black people, or of men and women, that would have implied two resurrections to those who are driven to cling to mere straws by the exigencies of a theory.

In coming to the New Testament, our attention is directed to the words found in Luke 14:14, "Thou shalt be recompensed at the resurrection of the just." The words were spoken to a Pharisee who was interested only in the resurrection of the just. In fact, Josephus tells us that the Pharisees believed in only the resurrection of righteous Israelites. We believe this is open to question, but be that as it may, this passage of Scripture builds no case for the dispensationalist. The fact that Jesus Christ tells the Pharisees that certain deeds will be recompensed at the resurrection of the just, is simply an acknowledgment of such a resurrection and the assurance that it will bring its rewards to those who merit them. The same significance may be attached to such terms as "a better resurrection" in Hebrews 11:35, and "the resurrection of life" in John 5:29. Professor Louis Berkhof rightly says, "These passages prove that the Bible distinguishes the resurrection of the righteous from that of the wicked and afford no proof whatsoever that there will be two resurrections separated from each other by a period of a thousand years. The resurrection of the people of God differs from that of unbelievers in its moving principle, in its essential nature, and in its final issue, and can therefore very well be represented as something distinctive and to be desired above the resurrection of the wicked."[6]

The words of John 5:28, 29 deserve more than a passing comment here. Dispensationalists quote them in support of two resurrections. The Scofield Reference Bible contains the prefatory words, "The two resurrections" at the beginning of this section. This is interesting when one remembers that what is written here is precisely what we have in Daniel 12:2. How anyone can interject a period of one thousand years into this passage is difficult to understand. If this truth be approached with an open mind, free from preconceptions, one would never suspect that it speaks of two resurrections, separated by one thousand years. Let us be reminded of its words: "The hour is coming, in which ALL that are in the graves shall hear His voice, and shall come forth; they that have done good, unto the resurrection of life; and they that have done evil, unto the resurrection of damnation" (John 5:28, 29). The Lord Jesus Christ speaks of "the hour." No spiritualizing or manipulating can make this hour to mean a thousand years. He is describing "the hour in which ALL that are in their graves shall hear His voice and shall come forth." All that are in their graves shall hear His voice in the same hour and shall come forth in the same hour. Surely, we have a right to ask by what exegetical athletics any unbiased student can get a period of one thousand years to fit into this hour? It cannot be done.

A statement similar to the above can also be found in Acts 24:15 where Paul affirms "that there shall be a resurrection of the dead, both of the just and unjust." How strange that in all his discussions of the resurrection, the great apostle never hinted to the early church that there should be either an earthly millennium, or two resurrections! It is frequently contended that I Corinthians 15:22-24 sets forth Paul's view of the two resurrections. The words are as follows: "For as in Adam all die, even so in Christ shall all be made alive. But every man

---

(6) Berkhof, Louis, SYSTEMATIC THEOLOGY, Page 725

in his own order: Christ the first fruits; afterward they which are Christ's at His coming. Then cometh the end . . ." The inspired apostle was writing to the Christian community in Corinth and explaining to them how the last Adam, the Lord from heaven, would restore the life which the first Adam had forfeited by his disobedience. This restored life shall not be subject to death, but shall triumph over it. It did this first in Jesus Christ Himself, who demonstrated His supremacy over death by His resurrection. He was the firstfruit of them that slept! The next demonstration of the defeat and abolition of death shall be given at the Lord's return when the dead shall be raised up. It is significant that the apostle follows this with the words, "Then cometh the end." Now the dispensationalist says, "Not immediately." Why not? Simply because that does not agree with the millennial theory which must be held at all costs. Surely Paul is a better judge of what he meant to say than anyone living today. We believe that he has said exactly what he meant. The fact that the apostle speaks much of the resurrection of the saints is not to be interpreted as an argument for the two resurrections. The resurrection of the saints was the only resurrection that had any significance or attraction for Paul, and this was true also in large measure of the people to whom he wrote his epistles.

Much importance has been attached to I Thessalonians 4:16 by those who feel certain that there, at least, the two resurrections are clearly taught. It is but natural that those who find two resurrections in other passages of Scripture should most certainly find them in this one. Let us examine these words which have been so often forced to yield a meaning which they do not contain. "The dead in Christ shall rise first," say our friends, "and you cannot explain that away." Now the fact that the dead in Christ will rise first certainly implies precedence for them over some others. Our problem is to find out who those others are. The dispensationalist says, "The others are the wicked dead, who will rise last." Now the words of this passage are sufficiently plain to admit of no confusion or misunderstanding. The apostle is not speaking of the unregenerate dead at all. They do not enter into this discussion. They are put in here by the dispensationalist, but not by Paul. What Paul says is this, "The dead in Christ shall rise first; THEN WE WHICH ARE ALIVE AND REMAIN shall be caught up . . . ." The word "first" is correlative to the word "then" which introduces as the second event, not the resurrection of the wicked, but the rapture of the living saints. If Paul believed that the resurrection of the wicked would be a thousand years later, what an opportunity he had for saying so, especially when he was doing everything possible to give the Thessalonian believers a true eschatological viewpoint.

In Philippians 3:11 the apostle Paul makes another statement which has been given a variety of interpretations: "If by any means I might attain unto the resurrection of the dead." Now it is well stated that surely Paul was not in any doubt about his attaining to the resurrection. If not, are we not to suppose that his anxiety here was concerning his part in the first resurrection? The context would seem to indicate that in this case "the resurrection of the dead" was used as a figure for some attainment in the Christian life to which the apostle was pressing forward. Dr. Moffat's translation of this passage is illuminating: "I would know him in the power of his resurrection, and the fellowship of his sufferings, with my nature transformed, to die as he died, to see if I too can attain to the resurrection from the dead. Not that I have already attained this, or am already perfect, but I press forward to appropriate it, because I have already been appropriated myself by Jesus Christ. Brothers, I for one do not consider myself to have appropriated this. My one thought is, by forgetting what lies behind me, and straining to what lies before me, to press on to the goal for the prize of God's high call in Christ Jesus."[7] It goes without saying that if Paul were actually speaking of his

---

(7)　Moffatt, James, THE NEW TESTAMENT A MODERN TRANSLATION, Page 248

literal resurrection from the dead, it would be unnecessary for him to add, "not that I have already attained this"; neither would he write such words as, "Brothers, I for one do not consider that I have appropriated this." The Philippians knew perfectly well he had not already attained to the resurrection of the dead. That is not what he was telling them, but rather that there is a degree of spiritual life which is yet attainable above and beyond the state of death in which he was then living. This observation seems to be supported, too, by the fact that here Paul uses a word for *resurrection* which is used nowhere else in Scripture. The Greek word for *resurrection,* everywhere else in the New Testamnt, is the word *Anastasis.* In this particular passage the word is *Exanastasis* which means *a standing out of* the dead. It can hardly be denied, therefore, that Paul's desire was to stand up and tower above the dead round about him (dead in trespasses and sins), and to be outstanding in consecration and spiritual power.

We have now examined the chief passages which presumably teach the two resurrections. There is but one conclusion which honesty and candour will permit. We have to state that there is not one passage in the Old or the New Testament that clearly and plainly teaches two resurrections, separated by an interval of one thousand years, with the possible exception of one verse in the twentieth chapter of Revelation. We have not examined that verse in this chapter as it will come under review in another. It would not necessarily mean that a doctrine is not true and valid because it is taught in only one verse in the book of Revelation. The anomaly confronting us here is that one can read the whole Bible without discovering an inkling of this doctrine until he arrives at its third from the last chapter. If, on coming to that chapter, he shall give a literal interpretation to one sentence of a highly symbolical passage, he will then find it necessary to retrace his steps and interpret all the eschatological teachings of the Bible in a manner agreeable to this one sentence. The recognized rule of exegesis is to interpret an obscure passage of Scripture in the light of a clear statement. In this case, clear statements are being interpreted to agree with the literal interpretation of one sentence from a context replete with symbolism, the true meaning of which is high debatable.

A decisive factor in determining the time of the resurrection is the true interpretation of the phrase *the last day.* In John 6:39, 40 Jesus Christ speaks of raising up His people at "the last day." In John 11:24, Martha of Bethany is reported as saying of her brother Lazarus, "I know that he shall rise again in the resurrection at the last day." Now, dispensationalists, having placed the resurrection of the wicked on the last day of the world's existence and history, will not admit that Jesus Christ meant this day as the time of the resurrection of the righteous. One way out of the dilemma is to suggest that He meant the last day of the church age. But it is dispensationalism that insists so energetically that "the church was a mystery first revealed to Paul." If this latter claim were valid, it would naturally clash with the other.

Some premillennialists, who have faced the insoluble problems involved in extreme dispensationalism, now place the rapture after The Great Tribulation, and call themselves "Post-tribulation Rapturists." They affirm that "the last day" is the day of the Lord. They hold that He will come for His church and with His church at the same time. "The Lord returns. Antichrist is slain. Israel repents. The sleeping saints rise. The kingdom comes with power. It is the last day of the present evil age, and the first of the age to come." Thus is the matter presented by one premillennialist. There are some observations there to which the amillennialist would heartily agree. The difference between the two schools of thought in this respect lies in their interpretation of "the age to come." The premillennialist, using those words, thinks of a millennial reign of one thousand years. The amillennialist thinks of the age to come as the consummation of the kingdom of God in all its glorious fullness upon a renewed earth where Christ shall reign, not for a thousand years, but forever. "The government shall be upon His shoulder; and His name shall be called Wonderful, Counsellor, The mighty God, The everlasting Father, The Prince of Peace. Of the increase of His government and peace there shall be NO END, upon the throne of David, and upon his kingdom, to order it, and to establish it with judgment and with justice from HENCEFORTH EVEN FOR EVER" (Isaiah 9:6). This is not a millennium of peace with a rebellion and a war at its close; but a reign that knows no end, and a peace that shall be everlasting. "In the days of these kings shall the God of heaven set up a kingdom, which shall never be destroyed; and the kingdom shall not be left to other people, but it shall break in pieces and consume all these kingdoms, and it shall stand FOR EVER" (Daniel 2:44). "Thy kingdom is an everlasting kingdom, and thy dominion endureth throughout all generations" (Psalm 145:13). One must at least admit that it is a tenacious devotion to a certain interpretation of Scripture which disregards those emphatic statements to the contrary, and limits the earthly reign of Christ to one thousand years.

If, as some premillennialists teach, "the last day" is the day of the Lord, we can turn to the New Testament for some information on what transpires on "the day of the Lord." Let it be said at the outset that the reader will search in vain for any word about the repentance of Israel at the last day. "When once the Master of the house has risen and has shut the door" there is no opportunity of repentance for Jew or Gentile. There is just as little said of a special resurrection for saints, or a delay in the resurrection of impenitents. "But the day of the Lord will come as a thief in the night; in which the heavens shall pass away with a great noise, and the elements shall melt with fervent heat, the earth also, and the works that are therein shall be burned up" (II Peter 3:10). This is Peter's version of what happens on the last day, the day of the Lord. Later in the same chapter he speaks of it as "the day of God, wherein the heavens being on fire shall be dissolved, and the elements shall melt with fervent heat. Nevertheless we, according to His promise, look for new heavens and a new earth, wherein dwelleth righteousness" (II Peter 3:12, 13). This is what shall happen on that last day, the day of the Lord. It does not suggest a millennium on the old sin-scarred earth; but a reign of righteousness upon a renewed earth, purged of sin.

The description given by the apostle Paul is in perfect harmony with that given by the apostle Peter. Dispensationalists say that when Christ shall come to be glorified in His saints and admired in all them that believe there will still be a thousand years before impenitent sinners shall be called out of their graves for judgment. What saith the apostle Paul? "When the Lord Jesus shall be revealed from heaven with His mighty angels, in flaming fire taking vengeance on them that know not God, and that obey not the gospel of our Lord Jesus Christ: Who shall be punished with everlasting destruction from the presence of the Lord, and from the glory of His power" (II Thessalonians 1:7-9). Might we not ask how it is possible to take vengeance upon them or to punish them with everlasting destruction, in the day when the Lord Jesus is revealed from heaven with His mighty angels, if they are to sleep in the dust for yet one thousand years after that event? If we agree with Paul, that when the Lord is revealed from heaven with His mighty angels, the wicked shall be punished with everlasting destruction, how can they be judged again at the end of the millennium one thousand years later, or how are they to be ruled with a rod if iron during the millennium?

What a contrast there is between this complex and confusing system of interpretation and the plain teachings of the Word of God! We are quite convinced that if people were to read no other book but the Bible, it would lead them to believe that the coming of Jesus Christ will mark the end of the world; and that at His coming He shall assemble all nations, and all individuals before Him for judgment. All the dead shall be raised. The Chief Shepherd, who knows His Own sheep, shall separate them from the goats. Each one shall go to the place for which he is fitted. Let us not be deceived; the Scriptures know and teach but one physical resurrection, and all the dead of all ages shall participate in it.

Chapter 12.

The Judgment

THE importance of the subject dealt with in this chapter demands that we acquaint ourselves with whatever truth God has revealed concerning it. It scarcely needs to be said that by the term *judgment* we have in mind the act of God by which He shall pass sentence upon all our thoughts, words and deeds, an act which is one of the important concomitants of the return of our Lord Jesus Christ, and one of the doctrines of the Gospel. This also is a doctrine concerning which reason is inclined to agree with revelation, for every man's sense of justice makes him feel that there ought to be future retribution and reward.

The doctrine of a final and general judgment has been held by the Christian church from the very beginning of the Christian era. It is to be found in all the Protestant Confessions, which explicitly affirm that there will be a day of judgment at the end of the world, but do not enter into details. The general idea was that the judgment would be simultaneous with the resurrection of the dead and accompanied by the end of the world as we know it. This view was held by the early Church Fathers who did not speculate much on the nature of the final judgment. It received more attention by the Scholastics of the middle ages; but the theory remained unchanged, with little or nothing being added by the Reformers. This does not mean that there were no other veiws. There were; there are today. For example: Liberal theology with its emphasis upon the immanence of God in all the processes of history subscribes to Schelling's famous dictum, "The history of the world is the judgment of the world." This suggests that judgment is a continuous process, and that a future judgment is unnecessary.

In this chapter our principal aim is to discover what the Bible teaches concerning the judgment, and to reassure ourselves of the Scripturalness of the Confessions of the church, and the Standards to which we ourselves have subscribed. The *Westminster Confession of Faith* in its summary of Scripture teaching on this subject says, "In the which day not only the Apostate angels shall be judged, but likewise all persons who have lived upon earth shall appear before the tribunal of Christ to give an account of their thoughts, words, and deeds, and to receive according to what they have done in the body, whether good or evil."[1] The teaching of this manual of theology is to the effect that there shall be one general judgment in which both fallen angels and fallen humanity will receive "according to what they have done." It is but natural that ministers and elders who have publicly pledged their allegiance to the doctrines set forth in the *Westminster Confession of Faith* should find themselves in a quandary when reputedly devout students of Scripture tell them that there is not in the Bible any suggestion of a general and universal judgment. One cannot dismiss with a wave of the hand the incompatibility of dispensationalism with the doctrines of the Reformed faith. That incompatibility may be the real cause of so many of our church schisms and secessions. It is but a matter of common honesty for a man to renounce a system with which he is not in full doctrinal sympathy and accord. The fact that in our day creeds are held in abeyance has opened the way, on one hand, to liberalism, and on the other hand to dispensationalism. It is, therefore, time that our creedal and constitutional articles of faith were taken out of the proverbial mothballs and re-examined.

Readers of the Scofield Bible will find seven judgments listed in its index. Some dispensationalists have not insisted on so many, but "no prophecy of Scripture is of any private interpretation" here, and our brethren are not quite unanimous as to the number of the judgments. It is well known that seven is

---

the number most commonly regarded as being the correct number by this school of thought. We have before us now a book containing twelve prophetic messages by twelve authors and bearing the imposing title of *Unveiling the Future*. The closing chapter of this book is on "The Fallacy of the General Judgment Theory."[2] This is very interesting indeed. It means that until now a great and influential section of the Christian church has been wrong and is wrong now in its interpretation of Scripture concerning the judgment. It also means that modern dispensationalism has discovered truths hidden from the devout saints and scholars of the past. We readily concede the possibility of such a discovery. The whole truth has not yet been received by the people of God, because of their incapacity to receive it. On the other hand, it is with absolute caution that we should think of accepting new theories as substitutes for the doctrines which the Christian church has held for nearly twenty centuries. This does not suggest that we should be bound by tradition. Our obligation as Christians is to follow tradition only as far as tradition follows truth. "Ye shall know the truth, and the truth shall make you free."

In our search for truth in this realm, it is but right that we should now present the view of judgment held traditionally by the church and set forth in the Confessions, and also the views held by modern dispensationalism. The former is merely that there shall be a day of judgment simultaneous with the resurrection and that the judgment will be for all. The latter theory is to the effect that the judgments are seven in number and their nature as follows: (1). The Judgment of Believers' Sins. (2). The Judgment of Self in the Believer. (3). The Judgment of Believers' Works. (4). The Judgment of the Living Nations. (5). The Judgment of Israel. (6) The Judgment of Fallen Angels. (7). The Great White Throne Judgment. The reader can decide for himself whether or not this plurality is "rightly dividing the word of truth."

---

(2)   Dunham, T. Richard, UNVEILING THE FUTURE, Page 150

The first judgment, that of "believers' sins," is said to have taken place at Calvary where our Lord took our sins upon Himself in His own body on the tree. That great transaction is not usually referred to as a judgment, but as an act of expiation and atonement. The second judgment is the natural outcome of the first. When man rests his soul upon the finished work of Christ, he becomes a new creature. He brings his life under Divine scrutiny and judges it in the light of God's word and God's holiness. As this is a lifelong process in the soul of every child of God, there is no real reason for placing it in the same category as the final judgment. It is but a phase of the sanctifying work of the Spirit of God within man, and to speak of it as a judgment can easily create confusion in the minds of those not too well taught and grounded in the truth.

The third judgment described by the dispensationalist is the "Judgment of Believers' Works." Belief in this judgment is said to rest upon Paul's words in II Corinthians 5:10, "We must all appear before the judgment seat of Christ; that every one may receive the things done in his body." Now it is clear that the apostle Paul did not say when or where this was to take place. There is nothing in his words to show that it is not a part of the general judgment. The dispensationalist says this judgment will take place when the church is raptured and is with the Lord in the air. This is the view that fits into the dispensational plan. It is correct to say that the Greek does not use the same word for *judgment seat* in this chapter as it uses for throne in Revelation twenty. In the former case the word *Bema* is used, while in the latter case, we read the word *Thronos*. It is quite clear, however, that the difference in the terms employed cannot justify the conviction that they stand for different judgments. The word *Bema* translated *judgment seat* actually means *a raised place mounted by steps, a platform, tribunal, used as the official seat of a judge.* (See Thayer's Lexicon, page 101.) The word *Thronos* has the same significance, but also suggests *kingly authority.* So closely related are the two words that in Acts 12:21 the word *Bematos* is translated *throne*. Herod sat upon his throne which was also the judgment seat. The difference in terminology does not warrant the idea of two different judgments.

The suggestion has been made that it will take God the seven-year period between the rapture and the revelation to judge and reward the works of His people. This argument is not impressive. It simply attributes human limitations to God. He has only to will a thing and it is done. It is also pointed out that it was to Christians Paul wrote the words, "We must all appear before the judgment seat of Christ," and that only Christians are therefore included in this judgment. His frequent use of the pronoun *we* is said to mean only this. Yet, this argument is far from being conclusive. Even if he is addressing Christians and telling them that they must all appear before the judgment seat of Christ, that does not mean that they shall be there by themselves. He is alluding to a universal judgment which shall be experienced by all men, Christians included. The burden of the evidence would seem to favor this view of his reference to the judgment seat. In the context he refers to "the terror of the Lord." We can hardly imagine that Paul would associate any terror with our Lord's dealing with the church "between the rapture and the revelation" after He has welcomed the church to Himself. The judgment, of which Paul speaks, has an element of terror for those who come to it without the necessary preparation; and it is because he anticipates that judgment that he persuades men. It is, therefore, the same judgment as referred to in the twentieth chapter of Revelation, in which the Seer of Patmos sees "the dead, small and great, stand before God . . . judged out of those things which were written in the books, according to their works" (Revelation 20:12). In each case the works of men are being judged. One passage says "all men," and the other passage says "every man." If dispensationalism still insists that not all men are included, and not every man is meant, then we say language has lost all meaning.

The fourth judgment in the list is "The Judgment of the Living Nations." This theory, briefly stated, means that at the Lord's return to earth all Gentile nations will be gathered before Him for judgment. He will divide them as a shepherd separates the sheep from the goats. "The goat nations" go to hell and "The sheep nations" enter the millenium. This theory is based upon Matthew 25:31-46. The footnote to these verses in the Scofield Bible says, "This judgment is to be distinguished from the judgment of the great white throne. Here there is no resurrection. No books are opened. Three classes are present; sheep, goats, and brethren. The time is at the return of Christ, and the scene is on the earth . . . The test in this matter is the treatment accorded by the nations to those whom Christ here calls 'my brethren.' These 'brethren' are the Jewish Remnant who will have preached the Gospel of the kingdom to all nations during the tribulation."[3]

A brief analysis of this theory will reveal that many questions are left unanswered. The location of this judgment is identified by dispensationalism as "The Valley of Jehoshaphat." This valley is, according to some encyclopaedias, a deep ravine, separating Jerusalem from the Mount of Olives. If this were to be an assembly of human spirits it is conceivable that they might assemble in such a place. At least no one knows how much space a spirit will require. Dispensationalism insists that "here there is no resurrection." This is a judgment of living nations; men, women, and children in their mortal bodies. Let it be remembered this judgment is only for the nations then living. The nations dead and gone will not have any share in this one. Besides this, there is the problem of space and transportation. Dispensationalism does not hint at the possibility of any supernatural process by which the living nations shall be transported to Palestine. A brother minister with whom we discussed this problem reminded us that this is the day of air travel. This is quite true; but if dispensation-

---

(3)   Scofield, C. I., THE SCOFIELD REFERENCE BIBLE, Page 1023

alists can conceive of any nation in the world having enough planes to transport its entire population to Palestine (to say nothing of all nations), then we can at least assume that the day of the Lord is still far off. It goes without saying that unless the world becomes tragically depopulated before the end, it would be utterly impossible to assemble all the Gentile nations of the world in Palestine, to say nothing of assembling them in a deep ravine outside of Jerusalem. We believe that all men will yet be assembled before God for judgment, but it will be after the resurrection when men shall have bodies which will be unhindered by considerations of space and distance.

The confusion engendered by this theory is further increased by the sheer impossibility of such a judicial act upon the part of the righteous judge of all the earth. Let it be remembered that dispensationalism teaches that this judgment has nothing to do with individuals, but with nations. This alone seems confusing, for nations are aggregations of individuals. It is impossible to punish a nation without punishing its individual citizens. Then, there is the difficulty of finding entire nations so wicked as to be destitute of any righteous individuals; or any nation so righteous as to be without unrighteous individuals. This condition is not conceivable before the end of the age. When Peter came to the house of Cornelius he said, "Of a truth I perceive that God is no respecter of persons; But in every nation he that feareth Him, and worketh righteousness, is accepted with Him" (Acts 10:34, 35). This means that the individual will stand on his merits regardless of the state of the nation. It means that the righteous man will not be consigned to eternal damnation for the transgressions of his nation. No man in his right mind would claim that America is a righteous nation today. Half of our people never worship God. By no stretch of the imagination could the other half be described as Christian. At the same time God has a remnant of believing people within this nation. Will any one insist that if the Lord should return immediately, the minority would be sentenced to share the fate of the majority, which would be everlasting punishment? When God was about to destroy the cities of the plain with fire from heaven, Abraham's momentous question was, "Wilt thou also destroy the righteous with the wicked?" The word of God answers that question very definitely. If it be said that the righteous shall have been raptured out of the nations before this judgment, it can also be stated that there are sheep, as well as goats, mentioned in the inspired description. Never in all of human history have nations been all sheep, or all goats, in the Scriptural sense of these terms. In the best days of ancient Israel, there were individuals whose hearts were not right with God. It shall be so until the end. The judgment of the nations is a judicial impossibility.

The proponents of this theory go further and assert that the "all nations" of Matthew twenty-five can mean only Gentile nations; the Jews are not included. The Lord Jesus did not make this exception; but this is the only thing that fits into the general plan. when we ask for a plain statement of Scripture to support this idea, none is offered. Here we quote the words of a dispensational writer: "Before Him shall be gathered all nations. This has no reference to individuals. God means what He says. The subjects of this judgment are the Gentile nations. This is no general judgment."[4] Now it is one thing to emphasize the fact that "God means what He says." It is quite another thing to assume that God means what the writer says. In this case God says, "all nations" but the writer says, "All nations but the Jews." We believe it was John N. Darby who said, "It is a miracle how people can read the Bible without understanding it."

When Jesus Christ commanded His disciples to "go and teach all nations," were the Jews excluded from that plan? We have just as much right to think so as we have to think they are excluded from "all nations" of Matthew twenty-five. It is quite true that in the days of ancient Israel those outside

(4)   Dunham, T. Richard, UNVEILING THE FUTURE, Page 100

the commonwealth were frequently referred to as "the nations." It is also true that this term is used in the New Testament to differentiate between Gentiles and Jews. This, however, is not a fixed rule. There are at least thirty-seven instances in the New Testament where the word "nation" or "nations" is used with reference to the Jews, or with the Jews included. Any one contending that the Jews are not included among "all nations" in Matthew twenty-five is assuming something utterly unwarranted. There is not a sentence in Scripture to prove conclusively that the Jews are not included in this judgment.

All who are familiar with dispensational literature will remember its emphasis upon "the rod of iron rule" in the millennium. We are told that in the millennial kingdom there will be wicked nations whose disobedience will require Divine discipline and compulsion. It is also being taught that such nations will be rallied by Satan at the end of the millennium and shall make war upon the saints of God. Does not this seem to be a contradiction of the dispensational interpretation of Matthew twenty-five? If at the so-called judgment of the nations the wicked nations are consigned to everlasting punishment, from whence come those nations who must be ruled with a rod of iron in the millennium, and who will rebel at its close? In Matthew 25:46 our Lord says, "These shall go into everlasting punishment." There is nothing to indicate that they shall be released from that state to populate the earth during the millennium. Dispensationalism teaches that the population of the earth will greatly increase during this period. Here is an enigma. The wicked nations are sent to hell before the millennium. The resurrected righteous reign with Christ. But, "In the resurrection they neither marry, nor are given in marriage, but are as the angels of God in heaven" (Matthew 22:30). Who, then, shall bring forth the millennial children to populate the world?

A further incongruity in this theory is the idea that human destiny depends upon human conduct. Dr. Scofield says of this judgment, "The test in this judgment is the treatment accorded by the nations to those whom Christ here calls 'my brethren.' These 'brethren' are the Jewish remnant who will have preached the Gospel of the kingdom to all nations during the tribulation."[5] Does it not suggest a departure from evangelical truth to say that the eternal destiny of men will be settled by their attitude toward the Jews? Since when has man's salvation, his heaven or hell, depended on any such thing? It is the acceptance or rejection of the Lord Jesus Christ that makes an eternal difference, and not our treatment of the Jews. A theory that makes the eternal salvation of Gentile nations to depend upon their behavior toward the Jews should certainly be popular with the members of that ancient race. Such a doctrine, however, is subversive of Gospel truth.

When so much prominence is given to the Jews in the exploitation of this theory, it is but proper to inquire whether there is any definite asurance that Jesus Christ was referring to the Jews when He said, "Inasmuch as ye have done it unto the least of these my brethren, ye have done it unto me" (Matthew 25:40). We believe that one can search the New Testament in vain for any such proof or precedent. The Lord Jesus Christ is reported as having used the term *brethren* ten times. In Matthew 12:48 He asks, "Who are my brethren?" The very next verse gives His own answer to that question: "He stretched forth His hand toward His disciples, and said, Behold my mother and my brethren! For whosoever shall do the will of my Father which is in heaven, the same is my brother, and sister and mother" (Matthew 12:49, 50). Surely these words are plain and definite, making the fact of sonship in God's family, and brotherhood with Christ, a matter, not contingent upon ties of flesh and blood, but upon a spiritual relationship to God. The same point is emphasized in Matthew 28:10 which reports the message sent by the risen Lord to His disciples, "Go tell my brethren that they go into Galilee, and

---

(5) Scofield, C. I., THE SCOFIELD REFERENCE BIBLE, Page 1036

there shall they see me." It is a fact, worthy of note, that the Lord Jesus Christ is not reported in a single instance to have used the word *brethren* to denote his kinsmen after the flesh. The Gospel writers employ the word *brethren* twelve times in referring to the children of Mary, our Lord's mother, but never has it been reported that our Lord used the word in that connection. On the contrary, He stated that only those who did His Father's will were His brethren. Let it be remembered that it was to Jews He said, "Ye are of your Father the devil, and the lusts of your father ye will do" (John 8:44). It is a matter for which we should all be grateful that our Lord Jesus Christ is above ties of flesh and blood, and that of His followers from all nations and tongues it can be said, "He is not ashamed to call them brethren" (Hebrews 2:11). We have never warmed up to the idea of regarding Jesus Christ as a Jew. He is the Son of man, the universal man, and God in man. Jewish nationals are not dearer to His heart than Japanese nationals: "For there is no difference between the Jew and the Greek: for the same Lord over all is rich unto all that call upon Him" (Romans 10:12).

The theory of the judgment of nations has been shown to involve insuperable difficulties. Many more questions could have been asked, which considerations of time and space compel one to omit from this work. If the dispensationalist insists upon an absolutely literal translation of these passages in Matthew twenty-five, he can hardly refrain from wondering how entire nations could have been expected to visit Jews in prison. If that be made the condition upon which a nation goes to heaven, we must conclude here and now that none of them shall ever get there.

Dispensationalism's fifth judgment is "The Judgment Upon Israel." This is presented in various forms. It is not stressed by all the exponents of dispensationalism, for some of them confine themselves to only four judgments. Of the fifth judgment, one writer says, "This judgment will take place on earth in the wilderness of Judea after the return of Christ in His glory, and will be for the purpose of sifting out the rebels against Jehovah and His rule. These will be kept from entering into the Land of Promise in connection with the setting up of the kingdom of David. Let the class study Ezekiel 20:33 and 34 and Psalm 50 for details concerning this lesson."[6] There is a transparent inconsistency here, and a contradiction of the dispensational theory that the Jews will be converted at the very sight of Christ on His return. Are we not told that then, "All Israel shall be saved?" From whence come the rebels against Jehovah and whence do they go?

If we do not like this presentation of the fifth judgment, however, there are other presentations. Another writer paints a different picture. Here are his words: "During the Great Tribulation period that will take place between the Rapture and the Revelation, Israel will pass under the rod. She will be brought into mourning and bitterness. She will be cast into God's melting pot. The Great Tribulation will be the time of Jacob's trouble. All of these visitations will be in judgment, and in their distress, and midnight of trouble, a remnant in Israel will call on the name of the Lord, and He will come as their deliverer, and will save them for the Millennial Kingdom."[7] Who can read all this guessing without lamenting the ᴖndless confusion caused by the dislocation of Daniel's seventieth week, which has meant the dislocation of so many other precious truths? Surely, truth is not being honoured in this mutilation which takes any passage speaking of a judgment and interprets it as a prognostication of a special judgment somewhere in the future.

Dispensationalism has not found a time nor geographical location for its sixth judgment, "The Judgment of Angels." It is simply said that the church will be associated with Christ in this judgment. "Know ye not that we shall judge angels?" (I Corinthians 6:3). Whatever the true interpretation of that

---

(6) Pettingill, W. L., GOD'S PROPHECIES FOR PLAIN PEOPLE, Page 44
(7) Dunham, T. Richard, UNVEILING THE FUTURE, Page 153

phrase may be, there does not need to be any doubt as to when this shall take place. Scripture is so plain and definite on that matter that only an inordinate affection for numbers would lead men to regard the judgment of fallen angels as a separate judgment. "And the angels which kept not their estate, but left their own habitation, he hath reserved in everlasting chains under darkness unto the judgment of the GREAT DAY" (Jude 6). The Great Day is the day of which Christ, Paul and others have spoken when all humanity shall appear before God's throne of judgment.

It is appropriate that the last of this series of judgments should be that mentioned in the twentieth chapter of the book of Revelation, and commonly called "The Great White Throne Judgment." Dispensationalism places this judgment at the end of the millennium, at which time all the wicked dead shall be resurrected and assembled before the Great White Throne. Now we cannot but ask whether there is any suggestion in Scripture that the dead of all ages will not be there. An argument to the contrary is built upon the words of our Lord, "Verily, verily I say unto you, he that heareth My word, and believeth on Him that sent me, hath everlasting life, and shall not come into condemnation . . ." (John 5:24). Now the plain facts are that it is possible to come to judgment without coming to "condemnation." The believer will come to the judgment, not for condemnation, but for vindication. This is clear from the inspired descriptions of judgment given in the Word of God. It is said that when Paul wrote, "There is now therefore no condemnation to them which are in Christ Jesus," he was referring to the judgment. Again, the same explanation applies. There is no condemnation, but there shall be a vindication and a rewarding of faithful service. Believers shall be openly acknowledged and acquitted in the day of judgment. We believe that the Scripture plainly teaches the doctrine of a general, universal judgment. Paul writes, "He hath appointed a day in the which He will judge the world in righteousness by that man whom He hath ordained . . ." (Acts 17:31). The Lord Jesus Christ likewise spoke frequently of *the judgment,* implying that there should be but one judgment, He said, "The men of Nineveh shall rise in judgment with this generation, and shall condemn it; because they repented at the preaching of Jonas; and, behold, a greater than Jonas is here. The queen of the south shall rise up in the judgment with this generation and condemn it . . ." (Matthew 12:41, 42). Here are striking statements. The penitents of Nineveh shall rise in the judgment with the impenitent Jews of Christ's day. They shall be present at the same judgment. It might be pointed out, too, that in that case, no one had the temerity to ask our Lord to which of the several judgments He was referring. He recognized but one day of universal judgment. This judgment is simultaneous with His return and the resurrection of the dead. In John 5:28-29 He says, ". . . The hour is coming, in the which all that are in the graves shall hear His voice, and shall come forth; they that have done good, unto the resurrection of life; and they that have done evil, unto the resurrection of damnation." In this passage the original word is *Hora.* It is the same word which our Lord used in John 12:27 when He was looking forward to that awful moment upon the cross where, for a brief period of time, the Father's face was turned away from Him; and in contemplation of the sufferings of that moment He cried out, "Father save me from this hour." There are other words in the Greek which denote *age-long duration,* but this word denotes a *definite* period of time. It means that there is an hour that has been definitely and irrevocably fixed and appointed by God in which the dead, good and bad, shall be resurrected and judged.

One writer states his objection to a general judgment in the following words: "The theory of a general judgment would reflect upon Christ's atonement and leave the recipient of the grace of God in uncertainty as to his salvation. We would fear to sing 'Saved by the Blood' lest after all we might be guilty of falsehood and presumption and be condemned for it at a judgment bar."[8] We wonder if it is conceivable that any Christian should derive his assurance of salvation, and his ability to sing of it, from any partcular theory of the last judgment? If any man is convinced that his brother who loves him as his own life is to be his judge in a law-court, that man is not likely to ask for a jury. He has all the assurance that he needs concerning the outcome of the case. Those who are Christ's have all the assurance that they need. "Herein is our love made perfect, that we may have boldness in the day of judgment" (I John 4:17).

We could find no more fitting words with which to close this chapter than the words of the book of the Revelation, 20:11-15: "And I saw a great white throne, and Him that sat on it, from whose face the earth and the heaven fled away; and there was found no place for them. And I saw the dead, small and great, stand before God: and the books were opened; and another book was opened, which is the book of life: and the dead were judged out of those things which were written in the books, according to their works. And the sea gave up the dead which were in it; and death and hell delivered up the dead which were in them: and they were judged every man according to their works. And death and hell were cast into the lake of fire. This is the second death. And whosoever was not found written in the book of life was cast into the lake of fire."

The dead are judged every man according to his works. Then there is something more. There are those whose names are written in the Book of Life and those whose names are not written there. The works which are being judged are simply the fruits and manifestations of the life which has motivated and governed the man. This spring of conduct, Christ in the heart, is not mentioned in the judgment of Matthew 25, but it is the same judgment. We cannot build a doctrine upon the details which are omitted in Matthew's description. In both cases, men are judged "every man according to his works." If this does not mean a universal judgment, what other expression would be adequate to convince those who seek further evidence? "The Son of man shall come in the glory of His Father with his angels; AND THEN HE SHALL REWARD EVERY MAN ACCORDING TO HIS WORKS" (Matthew 16:27).

Chapter 13.

Revelation Twenty

IT IS but natural that anyone whose eschatology differs from that of the dispensationalist should be challenged to explain the twentieth chapter of the book of Revelation, which is the very citadel and bulwark of premillennial eschatology. It cannot be denied that this is the chapter which suggests the plan into which dispensationalists try to fit all the eschatological teachings of the Old and New testaments. We have been somewhat amazed, and also not a little amused, to hear premillennialist brethren insisting that theirs is the only school offering any sane interpretation of Revelation twenty. All others are charged with either having ignored or spiritualized it, thus depriving it of any real meaning. We believe that a thorough acquaintance with the facts will reveal that every school of thought finds it necessary to spiritualize this chapter, and premillennialists are no exception to this rule.

Our present task is to concern ourselves particularly with the first six verses of Revelation twenty and to prove that they are capable of an interpretation quite in harmony with the position taken in this work, and quite at variance with dispensationalism. The dispensational and premillennial interpretation of these passages is that at the end of the present church age Satan is to be bound for a thousand years, during which time Christ shall reign in Jerusalem. The general assumption of dispensationalism is that the Jew will reign with Christ over the Gentile nations during the thousand years. The literal interpretation of the Old Testament prophecies will demand this, but no distinction between Jew and Gentile is found in the statement of the Seer who reports having seen, "The souls of them that were beheaded for the witness of Jesus, and for the Word of God, and which had not worshipped the beast, neither his image, neither had received his mark upon their foreheads, or in their hands; and they lived and reigned with Christ for a thousand years" (Revelation 20:4). There is no complete agreement among dispensationalists as to whether the Jews or the resurrected church will reign with Christ during this period. At the close of the thousand years, Satan is to be loosed to go out into the world deceiving the nations, mobilizing them for war against the saints. Satan is destroyed by fire from heaven and cast into the lake of fire. Then there takes place the final Great White Throne Judgment, after which the wicked are cast into hell and the eternal kingdom of God is set up. The amillennial interpretation of those same verses is that they began to be fulfilled with the first advent of Christ, and that the process of their fulfillment shall be completed when the Lord returns to judge the world.

The twentieth chapter of Revelation opens with a vision of an angel coming down from heaven with a key and chain to bind Satan. It is evident that the angel is none other than our Lord Jesus Christ, Who speaks of Himself as having the keys of hell and death (Revelation 1:19), and who alone could accomplish this feat. No other angel could attempt the binding of Satan, for " Michael, the archangel, when contending with the devil he disputed about the body of Moses, durst not bring against him a railing accusation" (Jude 9). The devil himself is a fallen archangel and great in power.

We believe that in seeking to interpret this chapter, one should try to remember that it was meant to have a message for the suffering people of God in that day, as well as for all the suffering people of God until the end of time. For this, as well as for other reasons, we believe that God led the Seer of Patmos to present here a brief summary of the entire Gospel dispensation, from the first advent of Him who claimed to have come down from heaven, until the second advent, when the kingdom which He has founded shall be established in all its glory.

It is our contention that the Gospels plainly reveal what is meant here by the binding of Satan. If we turn to the twelfth chapter of Matthew's Gospel, we find our Lord Jesus Christ claiming to have bound the devil. When the Pharisees saw Him casting out evil spirits they attributed His power to Beelzebub, the prince of devils. Jesus, knowing their thoughts, assured them that if Satan should begin to cast out unclean spirits that would be a case of Satan casting out Satan. If this should happen it would mean that Satan's kingdom should be divided. This was not possible. Having offered this rebuttal, Jesus then said, "But if I cast out devils by the Spirit of God, then the kingdom of God is come unto you. Or else how can one enter into a strong man's house, and spoil his goods, except he first bind the strong man? and then he will spoil his house" (Matthew 12:28, 29). It is plain to anyone that Jesus Christ teaches the impossibility of depriving Satan of those who are his subjects until Satan is first of all bound and restrained. That is what makes possible the salvation of any soul. Paul, writing to the Colossians, described believers as having been "delivered from the power of darkness" (Colossians 1:13). Satan does not willingly surrender his subjects. They are delivered from his power and snatched from his grasp by the superior power of Him who binds the strong man and spoils his house. When Satan is rendered powerless to retain his prey and made powerless to recapture his escaped captives the explanation is that he is bound.

There are many people who find it difficult to believe that Satan is bound today when there is such widespread evidence of his influence. Those who are spiritually enlightened are not ignorant of his devices. At the same time, we should remember that what we experience of the exercise of Satanic power is as nothing compared to the ferocity which he would pour out upon us if God should withdraw, or relax, His divine restraints and give Satan his freedom in this world. In the days of Job, Satan was definitely limited in his freedom to afflict the man of God. He is limited in his freedom to afflict every one of us, and that is why we are able to serve Jesus Christ.

The apostle Peter tells us that "God spared not the angels that sinned, but cast them down to hell, and delivered them into chains of darkness, to be reserved unto judgment" (II Peter 2:4). The fallen angels, which include Satan, have been already delivered to chains of darkness. This would seem conclusive, and yet, Peter says, "Be sober, be vigilant; because your adversary the devil, as a roaring lion, walketh about, seeking whom he may devour" (I Peter 5:8). He walks about as a roaring lion, but he is a chained lion and can go only as far as the chain allows. The chain represents a restraint and a restriction of movement laid upon the devil by one possessed of superior power. The Seer describes this restraint in exactly the same word as Paul uses to signify the bond of matrimony: "Art thou bound unto a wife?" (I Cor. 7:27). "The wife is bound by the law to her husband" (I Cor. 7:39). It is clear to anyone that this means freedom within certain well defined bounds rather than total immobility. Thus, Satan's freedom has limits, and while he is able to accomplish much, his sphere of activity is defined and limited.

The place into which Satan is cast is called the bottomless pit, or the abyss. This is his present place of abode from which he carries on his activities. This is a different place from the lake that burneth with fire and brimstone, into which the beast and the false prophet were cast, and into which the devil himself shall be cast in the end. This is admitted by Dr. J. A. Seiss in his *Lectures on The Apocalypse.* Dr. Seiss differentiates between the two conditions and says, "The relation between the two is much like that of the county jail in which accused criminals are detained prior to their sentence, and the state peniteniary to which they are assigned for final punishment."[1] Thus,

---

(1) Seiss, J. A., LECTURES ON THE APOCALYPSE, Page 270

according to Dr. Seiss, Satan is confined to a sort of county jail for one thousand years, and then to be let loose for a short period to carry on his pernicious work before being finally sentenced. We agree with Dr. Seiss that the binding of Satan for a period is not the same as the final doom of Satan, with the difference that Dr. Seiss assigns the binding to a future millennial period, while we believe it belongs to the Gospel age.

The casting of Satan into the abyss is a picture concerning which the human imagination has exercised itself with vigor and vividness. Dr. William G. Moorehead says, "Thrice is this undesignated pit opened, but when the dragon, the old serpent, which is the devil, is hurled into it securely bound by the angel's great chain and over him in that dismal prison the huge cover shuts down fast locked, and sealed, opened no more will it be till the thousand years are finished."[2] Here we have a vivid literalism. The place of Satan's abode is visualized as some sort of huge container having a lid upon it. The lid is to be sealed or soldered down so that it cannot be removed. We need only to pause to remind ourselves that here we have spiritual realities described in inadequate human terminology. Satan's abyss, or bottomless pit, is simply a representation of a state in which the descent and departure from God shall be endless, which offers no hope for all eternity.

We believe that the sealing of Satan confirms this view. The Scriptures tell us something of human and Divine seals. A human seal is not necessarily permanent. After Jesus Christ was buried, His grave was sealed by the Roman authorities. (See Matthew 27:66.) That seal was not permanent, but whatever is sealed by God is thereby made sure. It is instructive to notice what sealing means in the New Testament. The word is used of Christ Himself in John 6:27: "Labour not for the meat which perisheth, but for that meat which endureth unto everlasting life, which the Son of man shall give unto you:

(2)   Moorehead, Wm. G., STUDIES IN THE BOOK OF REVELATION, Page 133

for Him hath God the Father sealed." The word recurs frequently in the New Testament with a sense of authentication as when Paul's converts are called the seal of his apostleship. Circumcision was called a seal of the righteousness which is by faith. The word is also used of people appointed to a certain destiny. The Ephesian believers were said to be sealed by the Holy Spirit of God. That did not mean that they were confined to any place, but they were appointed to a certain destiny. Hastings' *Dictionary of the Bible,* Volume 4, page 426, enumerates certain ideas involved in *sealing,* such as, "ownership, authentication, security and destination." It says, "All these ideas, but especially destination, are present when it is said that believers are sealed with the Holy Spirit of promise." Now, if the sealing of believers is the guarantee of a certain destination, it is quite conceivable that the sealing of Satan has the same significance. When the disciples reported the triumphs of the Gospel, Jesus said, "I beheld Satan as lightning fall from heaven" (Luke 10:18). The preaching of the Gospel heralded and sealed Satan's doom. When our Lord finally died on the cross, He actually struck Satan's death blow, and is described as "having destroyed principalities and powers. He made a show of them openly and triumphed over them." The principalities and powers were definitely Satanic forces, whose doom were sealed by our Lord's death upon the cross.

Satan was restrained for a certain period and yet not altogether taken away. One of the chief prohibitions laid upon him was that he should deceive the nations no more until the end of the period symbolized by the thousand years, and representing the Gospel age. No other effect upon human life on earth other than the deceiving of the nations is mentioned. Nothing is said of universal peace or abounding prosperity, nor of the restoration of Hebrew economy. Satan is merely restricted in his work of deceiving the nations. It is an interesting fact that from that day until recent years, the Gospel has been having free course to all nations. At present, however, we have a different situation. There are nations being deceived by Satan, living in superstition and antagonistic to the Gospel, even passing legislation to prohibit its propagation. One wonders if this does not suggest the possibility that Satan is now being loosed for a little while to go out deceiving the nations which are in the four corners of the earth. The least that can be said is that few of our prophets could predict, even a decade ago, the present state of affairs.

John's description of the binding of Satan would indicate that it took place upon the earth, for he saw Satan's conqueror descending from heaven. The next part of the vision is in heaven: "And I saw thrones, and they sat upon them, and judgment was given unto them: and I saw the souls of them that were beheaded for the witness of Jesus, and for the word of God, and which had not worshipped the beast, neither had received his image, neither had received his mark upon their foreheads, or in their hands; and they lived and reigned with Christ a thousand years" (Revelation 20:4).

Dispensational brethren plead with us to interpret these words literally and remind us that the words must mean what they say. That rule does not always apply to the words of Scripture. Moreover, if we give these words a strictly literal interpretation, they might not say exactly what the dispensationalist professes to find in them. It is presumed that the words prove and teach the reign of the church with Christ on this earth during the millennium. Let us examine the words from the standpoint of a literal interpretation. The Seer saw thrones occupied by certain beings. We are told that the thrones are material thrones. Again, he saw the souls of those who were beheaded for the Word of God, and the witness of Jesus. Now let us note that he saw only the souls of those beheaded for the Word of God. Souls are not bodies, and further, the number beheaded for the Word of God is but a small fraction of those who sealed their testimony with their blood. The beheading must be given a literal interpretation according to the rule laid down by the dispensationalist. In addition to those souls the Seer of Patmos saw also the souls of those who had not worshipped the beast, nor his image, neither had received his mark in their foreheads, nor upon their hands. Here again, let us give the text a literal interpretation. The beast must be an animal, if we take the words literally. How, then say the dispensationalists that the beast is to be a man? It is pertinent also to ask how the dispensationalist insists that all Christians shall participate in the first resurrection and builds that doctrine on a passage which limits itself to those beheaded for the Word, and those refusing to take on their faces or their hands the mark of the beast? The remainder of this chapter could be taken up in pointing out the sheer absurdity and the great danger of attempting a literal interpretation of the book of Revelation. Instead of doing so, we proceed with what we believe to be the true message and significance of these words.

Let us for the moment allow our thoughts to go back to the first century when Roman persecutors were daily depleting the ranks of Christ's followers. If believers would be faithful, they must be ready to lay down their lives. The Spirit of God encourages such faithfulness and fearlessness in believers by presenting to their uneasy minds a description of the inheritance entered into by those beheaded for the Word of God and by their fellow martyrs in every age. They are not dead. They live and reign with Christ. Let it be remembered that John saw only the souls of those martyrs. Their souls lived and reigned with Christ, while their bodies rested in unknown graves, until the resurrection. We believe that this interpretation is supported by the vision recorded in the fourteenth chapter of Revelation. There we have a glimpse of the saints who "were redeemed from among men, being the first fruits unto God and to the Lamb" (Revelation 14:4). John is permitted to behold them in this unspeakable glory and at the same time he is given this heartening message to the saints still suffering on earth: "Write, Blessed are the dead which die in the Lord from henceforth" (Revelation 14:13). Let it be noted that it was after this that John saw the white cloud upon which sat one like unto the Son of man, who came thrusting His sickle to reap the harvest of the earth. These passages seem to teach that there is a heavenly state of bliss entered by the souls of those who die in the Lord, a state in which they shall live and reign with Christ until the time set by God for Christ to return and reap the harvest of the earth.

There are those who contend that the term *souls* is used in the Bible as a designation for *people* and including within its meaning both *souls* and *bodies*. An example of this is found in I Peter 3:20 where the occupants of Noah's ark are described as "eight souls." By this reasoning men seek to prove that "the souls" seen by John are simply people with souls and bodies. This is the position taken by Dr. Seiss. The Greek word translated *souls* is *psueke;* and while used in one hundred and five places in the New Testament, there are only five places in which it can possibly have reference to the body, and some of these five are debatable. This deprives the foregoing argument of any great weight, and would render it hazardous to build up a doctrine on the probability that it includes bodies. If we concede that the passage means people, rather than disembodied souls, the passage would then read, "I saw the people of them that had been beheaded," and such a reading would hardly do justice to its construction. The *Pulpit Commentary* states the case well in its homily on this passage: "Here is a vision of men from the earth, not men on it. That the expression refers here to men in what is called the disembodied state scarcely admits of question." The same volume also says in this connection, "The text indicates not that Christ came down to earth to live with them, but they soared up to live and reign with Him . . . In what state are they seen? Not in their bodily forms, but in the disembodied state."[3]

The foregoing would seem to justify the conviction that John actually saw, and described, the pre-resurrection state of

(3) PULPIT COMMENTARY, Vol. 51, Page 479

Christ's martyrs. We believe that it was this state which the apostle Paul had in mind when he longed "to depart and be with Christ, which is far better," and to which he referred in his second letter to Timothy when he said, "If we suffer, we shall also reign with Him" (II Timothy 2:12).

The disembodied souls of this vision lived and reigned with Christ. In the first chapter of Revelation, John describes believers as having been made "kings and priests unto God." This is their status in this present life, although their priesthood is more in evidence than their kingship. Christ has, however, promised a coronation and an enthronement beyond this life to those who are faithful to Him: "To him that overcometh will I grant to sit with me in my throne, even as I also overcame, and am set down with my Father in His throne" (Revelation 3:21). The saints in the Laodicean church have long since experienced a fulfillment of this promise, and have been joined by multitudes of others who have overcome and now reign with Christ.

The reign of these disembodied souls with Christ is said to be for a period of one thousand years. Dispensationalists insist that this period is to be interpreted as the earthly millennium with its duration literally for this length of time. It is quite obvious that the literal interpretation of a thousand years is open to serious question. The figures of the book of Revelation are admittedly highly symbolical. If we say that the one thousand years means exactly that period of time as measured by our clocks and calendars, what is to hinder us from adopting the same principle with regard to the other figures of the book of Revelation. We believe that the figure of one thousand years represents a definite period of time, measured by and known to God Himself. It is the cycle of time extending from our Lord's first advent to the day of His return. It consists of the period during which the souls of the departed saints reign with Christ. That is what they are doing now. This heavenly reign of theirs is described as "the first resurrection." It is with regard to this phrase that many people have become confused, for they think that a resurrection must mean the raising of the body. To be sure, that is the sense in which we generally use the word, but the New Testament speaks very definitely and in many places of the raising of those who have been dead in trepasses and sins to a newness of life. In the parable of the Prodigal Son, the Lord Jesus Christ speaks of the father who received his wayward son as saying, "This my son was dead and is alive again" (Luke 15:24). In John 5:25 our Lord is speaking of His power to quicken those who are dead in trespasses and sins. He says, "Verily, verily, I say unto you, The hour is coming, and now is, when the dead shall hear the voice of the Son of God: and they that hear shall live." We should particularly notice the expression "now is," for this means that at that very moment those who were dead in trespasses and sins were responding to our Lord's voice and coming to life. When the people marvelled at this colossal claim, Christ said, "Marvel not at this: for the hour is coming, in the which all that are in the graves shall hear his voice" (John 5:28). In the former passage He is definitely referring to the regeneration of the soul, which He describes under the figure of a resurrection. In the latter verse He referred to the physical resurrection. In Romans 6:4 Paul speaks of believers as having been buried with Christ and raised to a newness of life. Writing to the Colossian believers the same apostle says, "If ye then be risen with Christ, seek those things which are above where Christ sitteth on the right hand of God" (Colossians 3:1). In the light of these passages, one can hardly deny that Christ and His apostles regarded the new birth as a resurrection, or a raising of the dead. When this regenerated soul leaves the body and goes to be with Christ, the spiritual resurrection has reached its culmination, for then the redeemed soul lives and reigns with Christ. This is the first resurrection. "Blessed and holy is he that hath part in the first resurrection: on such the second death hath no power, but they shall be priests of God and of Christ, and shall reign with him a thousand years" (Revelation 20:6).

"The rest of the dead lived not until the thousand years were finished." While the followers of Christ were being slaughtered, and their souls ushered into the presence of Christ to live and reign with Him, there were others who were dying in various ways; but, alas, no such blessedness awaited them. They were neither blessed, nor holy, for they had no part in the first resurrection, not having known its beginning in the experience of regeneration, they could not know its end in reigning with Christ. They passed into the world of spirits to be kept under the power of death and to experience the terrors of the lost until the physical resurrection when their souls will be reunited with their bodies. The allusion to "the rest of the dead" implies that the Christians, whose souls reigned with Christ, were not living upon the earth at that time. These Christians were regarded as some of the dead, and existed in a state different from "the rest of the dead" who, while having a conscious existence, did not live in the same way, but will continue in misery and torment until the end of the cycle of time, represented by the one thousand years, when they shall be raised to shame and everlasting contempt.

It would be an allurement for us to comment on the remaining verses of this book as they point to the loosing of Satan for a little while toward the close of the Gospel age. We wonder if we are not witnessing this in our own day. It would be interesting to dwell on his final defeat and destruction, followed by the final judgment and the ushering in of the new heavens and the new earth. This is the prospect which makes the believer's heart thrill with eager anticipation. This concomitant of our Lord's return is a major phase of the blessed hope of the church. Restrictions of space dictate that we confine ourselves to the original purpose of this chapter, which has been to show that the so-called millennial reign of the saints and martyrs with Christ is a present reality. The figure of a thousand years represents the period during which they are to reign and live with Him, leading up to His return with them. We believe that when this point of view has been grasped it will not only eliminate much confusion of thought, but it will invest the pages of Scripture and its prophetic utterances with a new light and a clearer meaning for those who study the Word.

It may be objected that the day of the Lord will not come at the end of the thousand years if, at that time, Satan is going to be let loose. The loosing of Satan and the withdrawal of the Divine restraints by which he is now bound will be a feature of the closing of the age. This will be his last attempt, and will be put forth shortly before the Lord, with His redeemed, will leave His place in heaven. We may recapitulate and say that this is the vision recorded by John in the sixth chapter of Revelation: "And when he had opened the fifth seal, I saw under the altar the souls of them that were slain for the word of God, and for the testimony which they held: And they cried with a loud voice, saying, How long, O Lord, holy and true, dost thou not judge and avenge our blood on them that dwell on the earth? And white robes were given unto every one of them; and it was said unto them, that they should rest yet for a little season, until their fellowservants also and their brethren, that should be killed as they were, should be fulfilled" (Revelation 6:9-11). It was to be but "a little season" over and above the thousand years until the conflict of the ages would end with the final overthrow of Satan, and the establishing of the kingdom of God.

As an interpretation of Revelation twenty the amillennial viewpoint can be found even more reasonable than the premillennial theory. Many commentaries suggest the former as the only possible position. It is not accurate by any stretch of the imagination to say that scholarship favors premillennialism. One has but to think of the Hodges, the Alexanders, and Warfield of Princeton, and other outstanding theologians, such as

Lardner, Hammond, Hengstenberg, Hagenbach, Shedd, Glasgow, Barnes, Fairbairn, James Orr, Henry, Clarke and Lightfoot to see the inaccuracy of this claim.

One of the leading scholars claimed by premillennialism is Dean Alford. Much has been made of his famous statement on Revelation 20:4: "If in such a passage the first resurrection may be understood to mean spiritual rising with Christ, while the second means literal rising from the grave — then there is an end to all significance in language and Scripture is wiped out as a definite testimony to anything." While we accord Dean Alford all the respect due him, we are bound to state that we have heard a Roman Catholic using similar words while trying to prove the Scriptural origin of the doctrine of transubstantiation from John 6:54: "Whoso eateth my flesh, and drinketh my blood, hath eternal life; and I will raise him up at the last day." The Romanist says, "If this does not mean transubstantiation there is an end to all significance in language." He uses the same logic in interpreting the words of institution in the Lord's Supper, "This is my body which is broken for you." Dean Alford would not agree with this claim. In the sixth chapter of John's Gospel, bread is mentioned eighteen times. Six times it refers to the bread which men eat. Twelve times it refers to the person and work of Jesus Christ. In each of the eighteen cases the Greek word *artos* is used and with two vastly different meanings. In the light of these facts we are forced to dispute Dean Alford's argument for the two physical resurrections.

One interesting fact concerning Dean Alford which we have never found recorded by any premillennialist is that premillennialism never satisfied him. In his later comment on Matthew twenty-five he says, "I think it proper to state in this third edition that having now entered upon the deeper study of the New Testament, I do not feel by any means that full confidence which I once did in the exegesis here given of the three portions of this chapter twenty-five . . . I very much question whether the thorough study of Scripture will not make me more and more distrustful of all human systematizing and less willing to hazard assertion on any portion of the subject."

David Brown in his great work on *The Second Advent* quotes Joseph Mede, the great British premillennialist of another day. Mede, as quoted by Brown, says, "The rising of the martyrs is that which is called the first resurrection, being as it seems, a prerogative to their sufferings above the rest of the dead." On this statement Brown makes the following comment: "So far was he from finding all the saints in this vision, that it was with difficulty he persuaded himself that any more than 'the martyrs and the confessors, who were equipollent to the Martyrs' would rise before the last resurrection, and all the length he ever came was to be 'inclined on the whole to the opinion that all the righteous will rise during the course of the millennial kingdom.' "[4] These facts are not without significance. The men who are quoted by premillennialists as champions of their interpretation of Revelation twenty were men who themselves became less certain. Dean Alford became less dogmatic about it in his later years, and all that could be said of Joseph Mede was that "he was inclined to the position."

We are acquainted with keen students of theology who are premillennialists mainly because they believe that this was the eschatological view of the early church. They would be among the first to confess that modern dispensationalists are trying to support that theory by rash contextual mutilations. Let any discerning Bible student read much of the prophetic and dispensational literature flowing from the printing presses today and he will experience a reaction akin to revulsion at the liberties taken with the truth of God. It is about time the people of God discarded the unscriptural notion of the church's being secretly raptured away before the great tribu-

---

(4) Brown, David, CHRIST'S SECOND COMING, Page 223

lation of the end of time, of a remnant of the Jews becoming evangelists for the world, after the church is taken away and the Spirit of God has been withdrawn. It is about time we discarded the erroneous idea of a Palestinian Jewish kingdom with Christ as King. When His kingdom shall be set up there will be in it neither Jew nor Greek, but the redeemed of the Lord. When He shall rend the heavens and come down there will be no further opportunity for salvation, for then all the overtures of grace shall have come to an end. Until that day dawns, the souls of those who have slept in Jesus enjoy their millennium. They live and reign with Him now in glory until His return, when they shall appear with Him, in glory.

Chapter 14.

The Testimony of History

AN EARNEST and sensitive seeker for truth can very readily become prejudiced against any theory which he may discover to be based on mere assumptions. Inaccurate statements will ultimately do any cause more harm than good. For quite some years we have been told that the early church has been "Premillennial almost to a man." Many people will never go to the trouble of verifying these assertions, and for that reason they are accepted at face value. Those who will dig up the facts for themselves will discover that the facts do not warrant such positive and declarative pronouncements. A theory based upon suppositions cited as facts is bound to become reprehensible when the truth is known.

It is frequently argued, and not without merit, that the apostles and their immediate successors were nearer to the fountainhead of Christian truth than we are, and that this should give weight to their beliefs and doctrines. Whatever truth there may be in this statement, it is well to remember that neither the apostles, nor the church Fathers, have any right to be regarded as infallible, except as their utterances are inspired by the Holy Ghost. So prone is man to corrupt that which is communicated to him by God, that within a short time after Pentecost, Peter had to be sharply rebuked by Paul for having misunderstood his apostolic commission to the extent of compelling Gentile Christians to live like Jews. The command to go into all the world and preach the Gospel had to be endorsed by specific visions and directives from heaven before the leading figure among the apostles would condescend to show the way of salvation to a Roman centurian because he happened to be a Gentile. We simply make this observation to show that even the apostolic church was not a perfect church. If this statement be doubted by any one, let him read the letters of Paul to the churches of his day. Our pattern is not necessarily what the church has believed at any time, but what the Holy Spirit has plainly taught. This is not denying that the apostolic and Patristic church had Divine guidance in matters of Christian doctrine. It is but a reminder of man's proneness to taint the Divine with the human, and of the possibility that the church can be in error concerning a specific doctrine of the faith.

The beliefs of the apostles of Christ can be ascertained only by a perusal of their own written words. We have already devoted a chapter of this work to the testimony of the apostles, and now come to make a brief survey of the teachings of the early Fathers.

Students of church history will agree that if any premillennialism existed in the early church it was during the first four centuries of its history. It is a matter of common knowledge that after the time of Jerome and Augustine it receives little or no attention by church historians. This has for us the advantage of having less than four centuries of history to search for the required information.

The early church definitely believed in the second coming of Jesus Christ, and seemed to cherish the conviction that His coming was imminent. This latter fact would seem to eliminate the postmillennial view which expects a thousand years of earthly bliss to precede the Lord's return. Premillennialists have been quick to seize upon this as satisfactory proof that the early church was premillennial. To begin with, the early church expected the Lord's return, and there are many premillennialists who hold the erroneous idea that if anyone believes the truth of the Lord's return he must be a premillennialist. Inasmuch as postmillennialism was incompatible with the expectations of the early Christians, it is assumed that their only alternative was premillennialism. This does not necessarily follow, for it is a fact that all who believe the Scriptures must believe in the Lord's return and this does not necessarily make them premillennialists. We are not denying that there were premillennialists in the early church. In fact, Neander speaks of premillennialism as having been quite prevalent, but makes the following revealing comment on the subject: "What we have just said, however, is not to be so understood as if Chiliasm had ever formed a part of the general creed of the church."[1]

A cross section of the post-apostolic belief can be gathered from the writings handed down to us from these early times, notably the productions of the outstanding Church Fathers, such as Clement, Polycarp, Ignatius, Papias, and Justin Martyr, and also the writings known as "The Didache." These writings were reviewed by Professor Albertus Pieters of Western Seminary, Holland, Michigan, in the August and September issues of the *Calvin Forum* of 1938. Professor Pieters made a careful study of the writings of nine Church Fathers and was driven to the conclusion that only two of them expressed any definite premillennial expectations of the Lord's return. Dr. D. H. Kromminga, to whom we are indebted for this information, undertook to examine the same writings; and although a moderate premillennialist, he stated that he succeeded in finding only one pronounced premillennialist among these nine outstanding Church Fathers. This is a rather significant disclosure.

The Epistles of Clement held a high place in the esteem of the early church, for according to tradition, Clement fellowshipped with the apostle Paul. But we do not find in the Epistles of Clement any of the distinctive features of modern dispensationalism. He mentions the second coming of Christ, the resurrection, and the judgment; but has nothing to say of a restored Hebrew economy. The same can be said of the writings of Polycarp, who is reputed to have been a disciple of the apostle John. Polycarp looks for the Lord's return and speaks

---

(1) Neander, CHURCH HISTORY, Vol. 1, Page 651

of a resurrection and judgment, matters commonly believed in his day. Modern premillennialism cannot claim those writers, for what they have written is believed by every amillennialist. One searches their writings in vain for any emphasis on a Palestinian kingdom of which Christ shall be King. By no stretch of the imagination can one derive from them any suggestion of a rebuilding of the temple and a restoration of the Levitical sacrifices. "The Didache" is the title given to a very early church document supposed to contain the teachings of the apostles. It has much to say of the latter days, and predicts much distress and trial toward the end of the Gospel age. It speaks of the rise of a world-deceiver who will pretend to be the Son of God and shall commit unsurpassed wickedness. There are also suggestions of two resurrections, but no allusion to a thousand year interval.

The Epistle of Barnabas dates back to a very early point in Christian history. Lightfoot places it as far back as 70 A. D. Its writer was a native of Alexandria and not the Barnabas who accompanied Paul on his first missionary journey. Dr. Kromminga regards the claim that Barnabas was premillennial as "quite baseless," but points out the obvious fact that Barnabas showed acquaintance with premillennial beliefs, proving that such did exist in his day. Barnabas patterned his eschatological plan on the week of creation in the first chapter of Genesis. God worked for six days and rested on the seventh. The present world order would continue in operation for six thousand years; and the seventh millennium would be one of rest, holiness and peace, for "With the Lord a thousand years are as one day." The following statement from Barnabas gives some conception of his line of reasoning: "Behold, today will be a thousand years. Therefore, my children, in six days, that is in six thousand years, all things will be finished. 'And he rested on the seventh day' this meaneth, when His son, coming, shall destroy the time of the wicked man, and judge the ungodly and change the sun and the moon and the stars, then shall He truly rest on the seventh day." One thing Barnabas makes clear is that he is not a postmillennialist, for according to his point of view the coming of Christ will put an end to the present system of things and usher in the new age. Barnabas makes no mention of any special privileges for the Jews, nor does he hint at the releasing of Satan at the end of a thousand years. In fact, Dr. Kromminga remarks with his characteristic fairness, "The presumption that Barnabas was an amillennialist is decidedly strengthened by his marked and pervading antijudaism."[2] This is rather a striking admission from a premillenarian scholar.

Ignatius, the martyred Bishop of Antioch, was one of the greatest of the early apologists. He wrote a number of epistles, but has nothing definite to say about the order of events leading up to the end. It cannot be proved by his writings that he belongs to any particular eschatological school. Dispensationalists cannot claim him.

The second century produced two outstanding premillennialists in the persons of Papias and Justin Martyr. Papias was the Bishop of Hierapolis and reputed to have been a disciple of the apostle John. Eusebius, the church historian, suggests that it was Papias' close relation with the apostle that gave weight to his authority and caused many to be carried away by his opinion. An examination of Papias' eschatology takes one back into ancient Hebrew apocalyptic literature, and may explain the existence of premillennialism in the church while its membership was largely made up of Jews. The Jews of the pre-Christian era held a theory of a millennial kingdom. At first it was assumed that the kingdom would endure forever, and later the view became modified and the millennial kingdom was thought to endure for one thousand years, in accordance with the week of creation pattern already mentioned here. Thus the *Encyclopaedia Brittanica* in its article on "The Millennium" has the following to say of some of the early Hebrew

(2)   Kromminga, D. H., THE MILLENNIUM IN THE CHURCH, Page 33

Christians: "Accepting the Jewish Apocalypses as sacred Books of venerable antiquity they read them eagerly and transferred their contents bodily to Christianity. Nay more, the Gentile Christians took possession of them and just in proportion as they were neglected by the Jews who, after the war of Bar-Cochba, became indifferent to the Messianic hope and hardened themselves once more in devotion to the law — they were naturalized in the Christian communities. The result was that these books became 'Christian' documents; it is entirely to Christians, not to Jewish tradition that we owe their preservation. The Jewish expectations are adopted for example, by Papias, by the writer of the Epistle of Barnabas and by Justin."[3]

This is rather a significant charge, but one which is well founded. Papias' eschatological conceptions are preserved for us by Eusebius, the historian, but more especially by Papias' younger contemporary and ardent disciple, Iraneus, who reports them in the following remarkable paragraph: "The elders who saw John, the disciple of the Lord, related that they had heard from him how the Lord used to teach in regard to those times and say: 'The days will come in which vines shall grow, each having ten thousand branches, and in each branch ten thousand twigs, and in each twig ten thousand shoots, and in each one of the shoots ten thousand clusters, and on every one of the clusters ten thousand grapes, and every grape when pressed will give five and twenty metretes of wine, and when any one of the saints shall lay hold of a cluster, another shall cry out: "I am a better cluster, take me; bless the Lord through me!" In like manner the Lord declared that a grain of wheat would produce ten thousand ears and that every ear should have ten thousand grains, and every grain ten pounds of clear pure fine flour . . . And these things are borne witness to in writing by Papias the hearer of John, and a companion of Polycarp in his fourth book!" This was Iraneus' presentation of the millennial beliefs of his mentor Papias. But where did they originate! Papias did not receive them from John, but from the Apocalypse of Baruch, a Jewish book, antedating the advent of Christ. The only variation is that where Baruch says a thousand, Papias says ten thousand, for he might have reasoned that one was as near the truth as the other. This is sufficient to prove to anyone who will accept proofs that the outstanding premillennarian of the early church actually borrowed his theories from Jewish fables. Eusebius correctly states that the writings of Papias contain, "Matters rather too fabulous . . . which things he appears to have imagined as if they were authorized by the Apostolic narratives."

Justin Martyr, the other outstanding exponent of premillennialism among the Church Fathers, is not too consistent in his expressed expectations. He alludes to a kingdom which is not of this world, while at the same time he speaks of the rebuilding of Jerusalem, which shall become the seat of the Messianic kingdom, and in which believers, proselytes, patriarchs, and prophets shall enjoy perfect felicity for one thousand years. Justin Martyr has the following comment on the premillennial theory in his dialogue with Trypho: "I and whatsoever Christians are rightminded in all things are of this opinion, but I also showed you on the other hand that many Christians who are of pure and godly doctrine do not acknowledge it." Justin had the fairness to acknowledge that many Christians of pure and godly doctrine did not agree with his premillennialism.

It is a matter of deep significance that this millennial doctrine never found its way into the creeds of the church. Premillennialism did exist in the early church, but anyone who wishes to study the subject can find satisfactory proof that such premillennialism had nothing in common with modern dispensationalism. The early church believed that the Lord Jesus would return from heaven to set up a kingdom. Some people believed that this kingdom would endure for a thousand years in keeping with the creation week theory, but such a belief never met with universal acceptance. On the contrary this belief was associated with much heretical discord in the early church. Students of church history will remember the excesses to which Montanus and his followers carried this doctrine. The two prophetesses, Priscilla and Maximilla, associated with him, looked for the imminent descent of the New Jerusalem upon the city of Pepuza in Phrygia. The church found it necessary to issue a decree for the expulsion of the group from its communion. The movement spread to the west, winning converts in Southern Gaul, Rome, and North Africa, even carrying away such an eminent man as Tertullian. Much is being made of Tertullian's premillennialism, but the fact that he believed in baptismal regeneration and in the sin-remitting virtue of martyrdom is not given so much emphasis by the same sources.

The third century of Christianity saw the decline of premillennialism, while the fourth century witnessed its almost complete eclipse. The outstanding exponent of premillennialism in the fourth century was Lactantius, a tutor to Crispus, the son of Constantine. Dr. Kromminga links with Lactantius the names of Commodianus and Victorinus, but says, "After them no further literary representative of Chiliasm seems to have appeared."[4] Dr. Kromminga also points out the obvious reasons for the decline of the doctrine at this time. It was due to the rise of two of the greatest theologians produced by the early church; one was the learned Origen and the other, Augustine of Hippo. Augustine accepted premillennialism at first, but seeing its inconsistency he dealt it such blows that it did not come into prominence again for several centuries.

The doctrine was revived in Germany by the Anabaptists at the time of the Protestant Reformation. The city of Munster was taken over by fanatics who proclaimed it to be the seat of the millennial kingdom. The excesses and atrocities associated with that movement brought much odium upon the

---

(4)   Kromminga, D. H., THE MILLENNIUM IN THE CHURCH, Page 102

doctrine. None of the great leaders of the Protestant Reformation gave it countenance. It is amusing to discover in some writings the name of John Calvin given as that of a premillenarian. The great Genevan Reformer has left no doubt about that matter, and here we quote his words: "Not long after (the days of Paul) arose the Millenarians who limited the reign of Christ to a thousand years. Their fiction is too puerile to require or deserve refutation."[5] As a matter of fact, no theologian of repute advocated and championed this doctrine at the time of the Reformation. It is not contained in any of the creeds, and is condemned in many of the great Confessions of Faith. It is, however, approved by the Jewish Talmud; and that is the fountain from which it flowed.

We have examined this doctrine, taking not the writings of its opponents, but of its advocates, weighing the arguments in its favor by comparing Scripture with Scripture. In doing so we have been driven to the conclusion that if the doctrine is to commend itself to thoughtful students of the Word of God, it must be based upon a more impartial and more consistent exegesis of the Word. We agree with Alexander Reese, one of the premillennialists, who seems to see its weaknesses, when he says, "Millenarianism has need to pray frequently to be saved from its friends; for every cranky sect in Christendom — the Christadelphians and the Philadelphians, the Russelites, and the Crowdyites, the Sabbatists, and the Pentecostalists, the Winebrennians, and the Muggletonians . . ., all the mosquito sects that take themselves so seriously, and pester what they choose to call 'The Apostate Church' (usually all Christendom except a tiny sect); they all have their doctrine of the millennium, and do their utmost to discredit the vision of Scripture."[6]

Our examination of this doctrine in the light of the Word of God has established us more than ever in these truths which are the age-old heritage of the Christian Church. One would almost think that the parable of the wheat and the tares would

---

(5)   Calvin's Institutes, Vol. 2, Book III, Chapter 25, Section 5
(6)   Reese, Alexander, THE APPROACHING ADVENT OF CHRIST, Page 304

suffice to solve this problem. In it, the Lord tells us that the wheat and the tares will grow together until the harvest, and the harvest shall be the end of the world. There is no final separation, and no millennium of perfect righteousness in prospect before that time. The Lord's return will synchronize with the resurrection of the just and the unjust, the judgment of the human race, the destruction of the present world system, and the ushering in of the new heavens and a new earth in which righteousness shall dwell and from which every vestige of the curse, and every bitter fruit of sin, shall eventually be erased. This everlasting kingdom of His is not for only a thousand years. It shall never be destroyed. So until, and unless, it pleases the God Whose guidance and light we have sought, to convince us that we have been misguided, we shall cling to those truths, seeking to prepare ourselves and others for that great event to which the whole creation moves, the event which will forever seal and settle human destiny. "Lo this, we have searched it, so it is; hear it, and know thou it for thy good" (Job 5:27).

FINIS.

Index of Subjects

Index of Scripture References